BETTER GOLF
IN 5 MINUTES

J. Victor East

BETTER
GOLF
IN
5 MINUTES

Englewood Cliffs, N. J.
Prentice-Hall, Inc.

LIBRARY OF CONGRESS
CATALOG CARD NUMBER: 56–7001

First printing.........April, 1956
Second printing.......August, 1956

PRINTED IN THE UNITED STATES OF AMERICA

07369

To

My Wife

Elizabeth

Without whose patience, inspiration (and permission) this book would never have been written.

Just by Way of Introduction

VICTOR EAST, who is a modest and retiring man, wants to leave my comments out of his book. I am more than willing to let the publishers referee the matter.

Actually, the point of my "opus" is merely to record a chain of circumstances—havings its inception in the best set of golf clubs I have ever owned. In 1922 a man named Charles Warren Leland came to Chicago from North Carolina. He brought a set of golf clubs. Being "nosey" like all golfers, I began to handle the clubs. Never had I felt golf clubs like these—each had the same "feel," from driver to putter and in between. (Remember, this was in 1922.)

Learning that Victor East, at that time professional at Biltmore Forest, made the clubs, I sent him an order. In due time my clubs arrived, and they were even better than I had anticipated—they served me well.

In those days we put a more or less "balanced" set together by a process of trial, selection, and rejection. But East's clubs were the first truly balanced set I ever handled, and the results were excellent. The little changes he had made in weight—off the heel—or the toe —or the hosel—paid big dividends on the golf course.

About 1946 I played golf with one of the officials of the Wilson Sporting Goods Company. He had a new set of clubs they were putting on the market. I tried them. They had that mysterious "feel." Something occurred to me so I asked a question: "Is Victor East connected with Wilson?"

The Wilson man laughed. "Yes, he is helping us with our club designing."

Again the years rolled by. One day Arthur Marlow, British Consul General in Chicago, came to play at Chicago Golf and brought Victor East with him.

During our ensuing acquaintance I learned to know a most interesting man—actually a scientist of golf—in playing, in teaching, in coaching, and in designing. Back of those balanced clubs was a well-rounded, international experience in all phases of the game. All was leavened with interest, intelligence, clear understanding, and simple, direct approaches to fundamentals.

It has been a privilege to read his manuscript. Quite

apart from a unique and interesting story of world-wide golf activities, it contains the most understandable material on golf instruction that I have yet seen. (And I am a veteran of fifty golf books and who knows how many articles.)

East's instruction is not only the "how" of playing golf—it is the "why" as well. And the simple principles he sets forth so clearly actually "play" on the golf course!

Irving R. Allen
Member, Board of Directors
La Salle Extension University

Acknowledgments

AT THE OUTSET I wish to pay special tribute to the companies that, in my opinion, have made outstanding contributions to the improvement of golf clubs.

The first is the True Temper Company, which, through applied research, has made marked improvements in the playing characteristics of steel shafts.

The next is the Wilson Sporting Goods Company, which has done much to bring the age-old swelling and shrinkage of wood heads under control. With its Strata-Bloc material, Wilson has lessened greatly the ever-changing directional values that persimmon-headed clubs suffered under ordinary, seasonal changes in weather.

And, finally, is the Fawick Flexi-Grip Company, creator of the Golf-Pride grip, which, incorporating a lightweight material compounded of rubber and cork and a unique traction design that further lightens its weight, has raised the overall playing efficiency of the modern golf club.

In the preparation of this book much deserved credit belongs to Paragon Pictures, Inc., which took the photographs in which I illustrate the steps toward "Better Golf in 5 Minutes."

J. VICTOR EAST

Contents

CONTENTS

BETTER GOLF
IN 5 MINUTES

How Club Design
Can Help You to
Play Better Golf

*O*NE day the Prince of Wales, on a good-will tour of Australia, "cementing colonial relations," stopped at the Royal Melbourne Golf Club. I was the club professional at the time, and I watched him hit a few shots without much success. I went over to his equerry, Sir Godfrey Thomas, and said, "His Majesty is having difficulty with his shot-making, and he could quite easily be helped with his game." It wasn't too many moments later when I received a command to give him a lesson.

I suggested that we step over by a tree, just off the

course, and I placed several balls on the ground a few yards behind a low-hanging branch. I selected a club of adequate loft to raise the ball over the branch, and then asked him to concentrate on hitting the ball low and under the branch. He did so; and for the first time, he took a shot without making any attempt to scoop the ball into the air. He was forced to swing the way he normally would to keep the ball low, and the balls he struck arched out over the branch onto the course. I had proved a point.

Golf is a funny game. Here was a man having difficulties with one phase of the sport. I believe he would have done anything in hopes of finding a cure for his golfing ills. I don't know of any other game that so compels the player to seek perfection. Even as far back as 1491, the lords and barons of Scotland appear to have spent too much time improving their games. An edict from James IV, with pains and penalties annexed, ran as follows:

> Futeball and Golfe forbidden Item, it is statut
> and ordainit that in na place of the realme there
> be usit futeball, *golfe or uther sik unprofitabill*
> *sportis.*

This perfection-fever seems to grow with the game, as thousands of golf widows can readily testify.

Let your club do the work

I helped the Prince improve his ability to loft the ball by forcing him to concentrate on the ball and keep it low.

2

I proved to him that the loft is built into the club and that the same basic swing with the proper club would produce the shot he desired. One of my most prized possessions is the pin with the Royal Crest that he gave me as a reward for improving his game in one short lesson. I also received an open sesame to Windsor Castle if I should ever go to England. *The only thing that I had taught him was to concentrate on hitting the ball forward—trying, as he had been, to keep his left foot on the ground had nothing to do with lifting the ball.* I also might add that the following day the Prince beat Sir Godfrey eight up and seven to play. He had never beaten him before, he told me afterwards.

Before you head for the nearest forest to practice up on your iron shots, let me assure you that it won't be necessary. There was not enough time to tell the Prince the theory behind what he was doing. He was shown *how*, but not told *why* he achieved such a sudden improvement. You will be taught both the cause and effect, the how and the why, of improving your game of golf without the help of a tree. So hold tight.

It is difficult to point to any one thing in a sport and say, "This is the key." You can safely say, however, that *the key to good golf is in the club.* The proper clubs, coupled with a thorough understanding of how they should be most successfully employed, will help you achieve your best results on the golf course. The name "golf" is derived from the German word *kolbe*, meaning club. It seems only fitting, then, for club design to be an integral part of the game today.

A new driver for Bobby Jones

The game of golf, as dictated by the design in clubs, is quite different from the game of the 1930's and earlier. An experience I had in replacing Bobby Jones' clubs will serve to make this point clearer. Jones once asked me to replace his mashie-niblick and also to make a copy of his "Calamity Jane" putter, except for certain face imperfections. This led to a complete duplication of his entire set.

To give you some idea of the exacting detail required for this order, I shall confine my description of the work to the duplication of Jones' driver. This driver had been made by Jack White, one of the great club-makers of his day and winner of the British Open in 1904. Jones used the club White made (and I reshafted for him) during his "Grand Slam" of 1930, and it now reposes in the museum of the Royal & Ancient Club at St. Andrews, Scotland.

Although the exact reproduction of all parts of the driver was important, perhaps of more concern was the duplication of the "feel" Jones had for the club. Fortunately, I had previously reshafted this Jack White driver for Bob, and so knew the exact requirements of the shaft, both in its rough and finished state. Even so, I had to go through 5,000 pieces of hickory before I was able to narrow my choice down to four shafts. By test and measurement, these shafts were the four most likely to reproduce the playing characteristics of the original. The four "prospects" were fitted—not glued—to duplicate

4

heads. They were worked down to exact micrometer measurements of the original, weighed for duplication and tested for torsion, deflection, and recovery.

Of the four, two proved to meet the deflection curve of the original, and, since they also matched the torsion requirements, were processed into finished clubs. They were checked under various atmospheric conditions, and one proved to be the exact duplicate of the original in every respect. It became one of Jones' new set. I still have the other one as the memento of a pleasant task.

The hickory shafts of that day changed in torsion and deflection under various temperatures and atmospheric conditions; so every set–and indeed every club–was almost bound to be different from day to day. But, when the steel shafts were introduced, this variance between clubs was almost eliminated. Thus a modern golfer can depend on his clubs to respond in the same manner every day, no matter what the weather conditions are. Actually, when you step out on the course today, you should have with you a set of scientific instruments, each capable of performing a certain, specific job.

You're manipulating yourself right out of your game

Why, then, aren't we all experts? Most of our troubles stem from unnecessary manipulation. We use outdated techniques with modern clubs. When the kids are playing "golf" in the backyard with yardsticks and castoff balls, I'll admit they have to manipulate the stick to get the ball in the hole. But this same type of manipulation is not necessary, thanks to today's design in clubs.

Watch your partner the next time you approach a water hazard or a tall hedge. His natural impulse will be to scoop at the ball to help it clear the obstacle. He should make the shot with the same swing he would use to tee off. The necessary loft the shot requires is built into the proper club for that job. Any manipulation of the club other than having the sole parallel to the ground at the moment of impact is enough to throw the shot off. If the ball is not struck as the designer of the club planned it should be, all the scientific theories, the micrometers, the protractors, and all the years of study toward that one desired end might just as well be forgotten.

Points to Remember

- 1. The general direction and trajectory of the golf ball is built into the face of the club.

- 2. Your only concern is to swing in a simple manner to permit the club to do the work for you.

- 3. You cannot expect to play your best golf without the proper tools.

2

The Secret of The
Basic Movement

*O*NE of the great dif-
ficulties encountered
by golf teachers everywhere is that people learning the
game want to know immediately "how to swing." They
want to know at once about stance, backswing, foot and
leg movements. They ask, "What did I do wrong?"

As a result, golfers are taught how to swing and the
other facts of golf. Yet wherever you go you will see
players with rather "good-looking" swings which are all
right for clipping daisies, but which fail to produce satisfactory results on the golf course.

The swing is not the thing

The swing, important as it is, is merely the means to an end—to the effective execution of a fundamental action which insures satisfactory golf.

"Swings" come in all shapes and sizes, but only the swing that embodies *The Basic Movement* gets results.

A musical comedy once staged a number which called for the chorus to swing golf clubs. A prominent golf teacher was engaged to coach the chorus girls. In a short time he had them swinging the golf clubs in almost perfect form, rhythmic and beautiful.

But these were just "acted swings." *The Basic Movement*, which would have made these movements golf swings, was lacking. They were just "theater" swings—fine to look at but utterly ineffective on the course.

The Basic Movement *is the thing*

Effective golf requires more than just a pretty swing. The swing must incorporate one fundamental movement, *The Basic Movement*, that makes the ball go where you want it to go, whether it be a drive, a pitch, a putt, or anything in between.

Now *The Basic Movement* is unquestionably the heart of the golf stroke. Yet there is nothing mysterious about it, nothing complicated, nothing that can't be learned in a short time.

In fact, it is so simple, so logical, so easy to understand, that I can and will explain it to you in five minutes.

Five minutes to better golf

Not only can I explain it to you in five minutes, but, you can learn *The Basic Movement* in no more than five minutes of your own time.   You can grasp the principle of *The Basic Movement*, practice it, and be able to execute it in that short a time.   Then constant practice for equally short intervals can make it such a part of you that you will have a solid foundation on which to build your entire game.

When you have *The Basic Movement* clearly in your mind—and in your hands—if you so desire, you will find that your present swing will produce results you never thought possible.   And it will quickly, and increasingly, give you better, straighter shots with every club in your bag.   Then it will really pay off in consistently lower scores in actual play.

Remember, the swing as such is only the means to an end.   And that end is the simplest and most effective application of *The Basic Movement* that all good players, consciously or unconsciously, employ in striking the ball with the club face—the action on which all successful golf shots are based.

The Basic Movement—*the heart of successful golf*

Everything that takes place in the golf swing is designed and aimed toward one thing—*to take the face of the club "through" the ball;* that is:

9

(1) The face of the club must go "through" the ball.

(2) The face must be square on the target.

(3) The club head must graze the ground.

And this, essentially, is what *The Basic Movement* comprises.

A good marksman points the gun muzzle correctly and then squeezes the trigger gently so as not to disturb his aim.   All else is secondary.

The expert golfer brings the *bottom edge* of his club *squarely* to the line of flight *along the ground* for the few inches in which the club sends the ball.

After long years, it has been proved that any swing that properly embodies *The Basic Movement* will send the ball straight and as far as the physical ability of the player permits.

Why **The Basic Movement** *works for you*

The Basic Movement has been the heart and core of golf since the game began—before players knew or wanted to know *how* to hit the ball.

The mechanics of *The Basic Movement* are the direct result of the design of the golf clubs themselves. Thus, when you understand these principles, you will see why you should make *The Basic Movement* the basis for your own game:

(1) **The pitch or "loft" of the club head is what raises the ball.** *The elevation of the ball is built into the club.*

(2) **Therefore, all *you* need to control is the *direction* and *distance* of the shot.**

(3) **The bottom edge of the club is your sight for aiming—it must go through in line with and square to the direction you want.**

(4) **The club travels at ground level at and after impact in the line of direction desired.**

These points are the key to *every* successful golf shot —from drive to putt and all the others in between. You will understand, then, what a great British golf teacher meant when he said, "I play straight ahead—I play straight ahead *along the ground.*"

What I learned from "The Texas Swing"

Many, many years ago most teachers would place several tees on the ground *ahead of the ball in its line of flight*. When the pupil could knock down all the tees on his follow-through, he hit the ball, *after* he had acquired

11

The Basic Movement, which this procedure brought about. Many minds, many versions—all to the same end.

Willie Macfarlane in a practice round with Olin Dutra prior to the Open Championship at Merion in 1934, said, "Olin, you are quitting at the ball." Heeding Willie's advice, Olin resumed execution of *The Basic Movement*, went on, and won the championship.

A friend of mine, when his game goes wrong says, "Guess I'll go back to the 'Texas swing.' " And he immediately begins to hit the ball. He explains:

> Playing in Texas with a pro, there was one hole that always knocked me out. The second shot was a wood across a creek—with a steep, high bank on the far side and the green up topside. I invariably drove my ball into the bank short of the green—couldn't get it up.
>
> One day the pro with whom I played asked, "Will you try something?"
>
> I said, "I'll try anything!"
>
> He said, "See that little bush on the far side of the creek, right at the water's edge? Well, this time—letting the club sole naturally—*try to drive the ball into the low bush!*"
>
> I did as he said. And the ball took a beautiful high flight and dropped on the green. So ever since, when my swing goes sour, I go back to the "Texas swing"—and the skies are blue again.

Well, the methods—the thought—may differ, but all are designed to produce the same result.

**How you can learn The Basic Movement
in five one-minute steps**

Now we come to the heart of the matter—how *you* can learn *The Basic Movement*. It will take you only five one-minute sections to understand and absorb the fundamentals that can make *The Basic Movement* part of your own standard golf equipment:

The Five-minute Plan

First Minute

Begin by trying to *brush* the *sole* of a golf club *squarely* along the floor, grass, or other level surface *for about three inches*. Do this with a half swing; never mind *how* you swing—just keep brushing the surface squarely until you get the feel of it.

Second Minute

You will probably find that the front or back of the club *bumps* the ground. Correct this so that there is a smooth, bumpless stroke for the three or four inches of contact.

Third Minute

Keep practicing until the bumping ceases and the sole of the club is swinging smoothly along, flush with the surface. Then *do the same thing, making a full swing.* Don't think about *how* you swing—just concentrate on carrying out *The Basic Movement.*

Fourth Minute

Practice so that *control will pass from sight to feel—and to feel alone,* which is the proper way to meet the ball. Think about only one thing—making *The Basic Movement* part of your reflex action, with the sole of the club squarely grazing at and beyond the spot where the ball would be placed.

Fifth Minute

After you get the feel, imagine that you have a ball down on the surface to be hit. Strike at it as though you intended to send it along the ground. That's the whole story in a nutshell. The swing alone is not the thing—the correct production of *The Basic Movement* is the *one thing* that will better your golf game immediately.

THE SECRET OF THE BASIC MOVEMENT

Remember, to get the ball UP, you must swing the club sole ALONG THE GROUND. The built-in elevation in the club will take the ball upwards for you.

How to prove to yourself that The Basic Movement *works*

Before anything can be accepted fully by the subconscious mind, a conviction that it is sound and right must be established. Here is a simple way to make your subconscious mind understand and have complete faith in what *The Basic Movement* does with the golf ball—in how simply and effectively the ball will rise in the air when "played along the ground."

You can try indoors or outdoors. The illustrations show it being done indoors and warrant serious study.

If you try it indoors, a book and easy chair are your "props." If outdoors, a ball box on end will serve the purpose.

Here's what you do

Take your No. 9 iron. Square the sole to the ground, aiming with the bottom edge only—that is your gauge to the line you want. Now graze the ground back and forth with the club in *The Basic Movement*.

The ball rises and carries over the book into the armchair. No lift, scoop, twist, or turn—just the square-faced grazing of the sole of the club.

How to Get the Ball in the Air

*(1) Take your No. 9 iron. Square the sole to the
ground, aiming with the bottom edge only.*

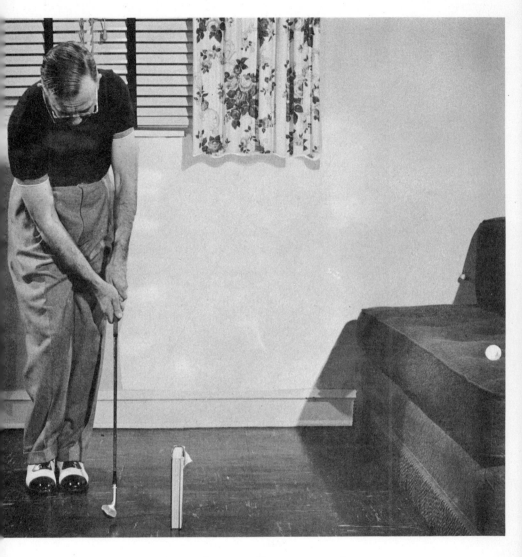

HOW TO GET THE BALL IN THE AIR

(2) Note how in the forward stroke the hands have moved forward. This is of basic importance since it has permitted the club face loft to raise the ball over the book as shown.

17

How to Get the Ball in the Air

(3) This picture of the wrong *way is shown to emphasize the faulty hand-scooping action, which at best produces overspin, instead of backspin, on the ball.*

If you do scoop, lift, or twist, the ball will hit the book. Only the correct *Basic Movement* will give you the benefit of the built-in lofting power of the club.

Note especially in the pictures the position of the hands after meeting the ball. It's the *forward movement* of hands, arms, and body weight that keeps the club low.

When you have fully mastered the fundamental principles and made *The Basic Movement* part of your muscular habit, then you have acquired something that works with every club in the bag—on weekdays and Sundays— whether you are playing for fun or for money. And it doesn't take long—you will notice the improvement immediately.

Points to Remember

- 1. A pretty swing is not enough— it must incorporate *The Basic Movement* to be effective.

- 2. The proper lofting power is built into each golf club—all *you* need to control is the direction and distance of your shot.

- 3. The heart of good golf is *The Basic Movement*—bringing the bottom edge of the club squarely to the line of flight along the ground for the few inches in which the club sends the ball.

- 4. Make *The Basic Movement* part of your muscular reflex action. First, prove to yourself that it works by the simple method described. Then practice the five-minute plan until you have *The Basic Movement* down pat.

3

Fitting the Club
to the Player

*G*OLF, unlike few other sports, is an individual game. The golfer is required to hit a stationary ball, and the distance and direction he gets with his shots determine his success or failure. The manner in which the ball is struck, or the swing, is the integral part of the game. Any experienced golfer can tell you that no two players develop swings exactly alike in every respect. It might seem that a majority of players would require clubs made to order, to compensate for these individual differences. But this is not generally the case.

What *is* necessary is a careful selection of factory-made clubs that fit the individual. There is nothing so personal to a golfer as his clubs.

Do your clubs fit you?

Several years ago I conducted a little experiment to prove my point on the importance of individual club design. The hammer is a tool with which most people are familiar, and it is designed, like a golf club, to represent an extension of the hands. I took two hammers, identical in shape and weight, and had their faces ground off very slightly in opposite directions. I partially drove two nails, in upright positions, into a block of wood and took the block to a carpenter. I didn't choose just any carpenter—this man had been making packing cases for almost thirty years. "John," I said, "just as an experiment, I want you to give these nails a straight drive with these hammers—one nail with one hammer and the other nail with the other hammer." I handed him one of the hammers with the face ground at a slight angle.

The nail he first struck went askew in one direction. The other nail angled off in the opposite direction when he struck it with the other hammer. Now, if an expert carpenter cannot drive a nail straight with a faulty hammer, *how can golfers expect to hit the ball straight with imperfectly made clubs?*

They can't. To give you a brief idea of the exacting requirements of the clubs that accompany a successful professional golfer, I call your attention to part of my worksheet on Bobby Jones' driver and brassy, which appears on pages 24 and 25.

There is a set of factory-made clubs to fit you

Today's factory-made clubs are designed to fit a maximum number of people. Clubs really don't have to vary too much from an average size. You can take, for example, a small person five feet, six inches tall and compare him to a person of six feet, six inches. Although on the surface one is taller than the other, the differences in the lengths of their clubs won't be so noticeable. The length of clubs is determined from a hands-to-ground distance; and in these two individuals that difference will not exceed a couple of inches. Unless you have an extremely abnormal build, the modern factory can provide you with a set of clubs that will fit you reasonably well.

You can't, however, step into a pro shop or a sports store and select a set of clubs haphazardly. There are a few fundamental measurements that you or your professional must be aware of before you make your purchase. Otherwise your requirements with regards to lofts, lies, shafts, grips, and club weights may be off to some degree. When you consider the possibilities, it is no small wonder that occasional sour shots mar some people's games. Many swings contain compensations for faulty design as far as the individual is concerned.

Where does that leave you? Either you are now

OWNER	Club	Shaft	Shaft Deflections	P-O-B	Swing Balance	Weight	Length	Loft
ROBT. T. JONES	DR	H-R	93–105–46–89	12½"	5 oz.	13¼ oz.	43³⁄₁₆"	8°
OUR COPY No. 1	"	"	"	"	"	"	"	"
ROBT. T. JONES	BR	H-R-W	93–105–51–97	12⁹⁄₁₆"	"	"	42½"	11°
OUR COPY	"	"	95–105–51–98	"	"	"	"	"

OWNER	Facing H-or-S	Lie	Face at Zero	Face Curvature	Right or Left	Face Depth and Length
ROBT. T. JONES (Cont.)	2½° H	53½°	15⁄16"	³⁄₆₄" x ³⁄₃₂"	⅛" L	1½" x 2⅞"
OUR COPY No. 1 (Cont.)	"	"	"	"	"	"
ROBT. T. JONES (Cont.)	0	"	13⁄16"	1⁄16" x ³⁄₆₄"	"	1¹⁵⁄₃₂" x 2¾"
OUR COPY (Cont.)	"	"	"	"	"	"

SHAFT SIZES

OWNER	Head Depth and Width	6"	16"	26"	At Grip	At Top	Grip Length
ROBT. T. JONES (Cont.)	1 11/16" x 3 1/16"	.48"	.55"	.63"	.65"	.74"	12¾"
OUR COPY No. 1 (Cont.)	"	.47"	.56"	"	"	"	"
ROBT. T. JONES (Cont.)	1 9/16" x 2 25/32"	.48"	.53"	.51"	.63"	.75"	13"
OUR COPY (Cont.)	"	"	.54"	.50"	"	"	"

GRIP SIZES

OWNER	0"	1"	3"	6"	9"	12"	Grip Kind
ROBT. T. JONES (Cont.)	.81"	.81"	.81"	.78"	.74"	.73"	Gusset
OUR COPY No. 1 (Cont.)	"	"	"	"	"	"	"
ROBT. T. JONES (Cont.)	"	.83"	.80"	.77"	"	"	"
OUR COPY (Cont.)	"	"	"	"	"	"	"

SHAFT CHOSEN FOR DUPLICATION

Kind	Weight	Deflection
H-R	7⅛ oz.	96–107–41–71
H-R-W	7¼ oz.	96–107–44–78

delighted at having found something new to blame for your poor showing last week, or you are gazing with regret at the bill for your newest set of clubs. Before you let either trend of thought develop into something serious, give heed to the following fundamental measurements that must be right.

Flexibility of shafts and weight of club head

The speed of your swing determines the weight of the club head and the proper flexibility of shaft for that club. A shaft too whippy for your swing reduces your driving power and costs you distance. Your golf professional knows from the figures you give him the proper flexibility of shaft for each club. Determining proper shaft flexibility is not so complex or confusing as most golfers think to be the case, for usually it narrows down to temperament. If you are a strong person, the shaft had best be on the firm or stiff side, with the club weight correspondingly heavier than medium. Conversely, if you are a lightly built person, you will find it easier to use a flexible shafted club of lighter overall weight. A quick talker is almost bound to be a fast club-swinger. Therefore, such a player, knowing that the tempo of the stroke must be in smooth progression, selects a club with a firm and not a whippy shaft. Also such a person should use a heavier club. We can apply the same reasoning to each type of individual. The age of the golfer must be considered, for, along with any slowing down of muscular effort, lighter-weight clubs with increased flexibility of

shafts are usually helpful and are accordingly prescribed.

Length of shafts and correct club lie

The shafts of your clubs should be exactly the length
that you can swing comfortably . . . no more . . . no
less. Within proper limits, we know a longer club will
produce greater speed at the point of impact. Greater
speed gives greater distance, but don't sacrifice accuracy
in obtaining distance. It is the matter of reach or relative
distance to the ground that is important in fitting an individual with the length of club he can best use. When
you bring your hands together to grip the club, it is the
distance between them and the ball that has to be accom-
modated by the club length. As I mentioned before, the
comparatively slight difference in hands-to-ground distance between tall and short people accounts for the narrow range in club lengths used by short and tall players.

The next point to consider in length-fitting clubs is
the club lie. Obviously, if you play the ball a long way
from the feet, you will need a longer shaft than you would
need if you should stand closer to the ball.

Since the distance of hands to ground and the lie of
a club are essential to length-fitting, it is of first importance
to study the stature of each individual. Your build will
determine the type of swing best suited for you—upright,
medium, or flat.

Once typed for the kind of swing best suited to your
build, the length-lie fitting procedure should go according to the following plan:

27

(1) Take an accommodating, well-balanced position, with your feet about shoulder width apart.

(2) Extend both arms and bring both hands in front of you.

(3) Slide one hand up and the other down.

Your professional should then place a length-lie recorder, if he has one, between your hands. This will help him determine the correct length and lie for your body and stance. (This length-lie recorder is a club head with a hinged shaft. The lie can be adjusted to the individual's preference, and the length can be read from the tape that goes up the shaft.)

Since the lie of the club is so important, it perhaps would be wise to point out that, when a club is held in the position of address to a ball by the person being fitted, the sole of the club should rest on the heel side of the center. Any golf club, when swung, changes to a flatter lie than when it is held in the stationary position of address to the ball. Therefore, never should a club be selected where the sole is resting at center or forward of center when the club is held in the position of ball address.

Test the adequacy of your clubs

Now it is rarely necessary for you to get individually or personally designed clubs. With the aid of your professional you should be able to select a set of reputable factory-made clubs that will serve you well. He may ask

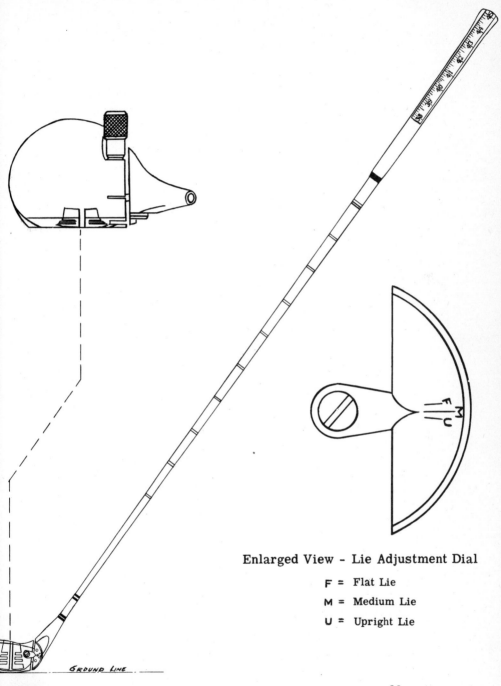

GROUND LINE

Enlarged View - Lie Adjustment Dial

F = Flat Lie

M = Medium Lie

U = Upright Lie

29

you to fill out a form similar to the one that follows. How well do you score on this questionnaire? If you find that you're scoring poorly, your next step might be to buy a new set of clubs—clubs designed to help you play better golf.

You and Your Clubs

The answers to these questions will be of key importance to your club professional when he helps you select your clubs and analyze your game. The reasons and possible explanations of your answers follow on the next page.

1. What is your age?
2. What is your height? Reach? Weight?
3. What is your glove size? Or give an outline sketch of outstretched hand.
4. What is the distance from closed knuckles to floor when you are standing erect?
5. How long have you played? Your handicap? Or average score?
6. Do you play with wood-shafted clubs?
7. Do you play with steel-shafted clubs?
8. What make of clubs do you use? What year did you get them?
9. Do you use a No. 1 wood to drive? A No. 2? A No. 3 or 4?
10. What is the length of your driving club? Weight?
11. How do the scratch marks run on the sole of your driving club? Are they straight or curved? How long are they? Do they curve toward the toe or the heel?
12. Where is the lacquer or varnish worn off the sole? Is it evenly worn? Is it worn more off the toe than the heel?
13. Do you have blisters or sore hands after playing?
14. Can you close your eyes and bring your driver into true striking position six inches or so from the floor?
15. Do you, or did you, play baseball or tennis?
16. How long would it normally take you to walk a quarter of a mile?

You and Your Clubs (Cont.)

Analysis of Answers

1–8. These are physical requirements that will require specific answers. Your general body strength, size, and ability as a golfer must be considered in fitting clubs to your individual needs. These answers will help in determining the flexibility of your shafts and the length-lie fitting of your clubs. See your club professional.

9. If you do not use the No. 1 wood for driving, this fact indicates a faulty grip. You are probably reducing the loft while you're taking your shot. Using a 3 or 4 wood to drive indicates a much more serious grip fault than if you consistently use the 2.

10. You may be using a club too heavy or light, or too long or short, depending on the answer you gave to Question 11.

11. If the scratch marks are square with the face and run from the front to the back edge of the sole, you have nothing to worry about. Even if they run for one inch or so and then curve, you're not in too much trouble. But if the scratches are not straight for at least an inch, what you are probably doing is instinctively making up for a faulty grip at the same time you make contact with the ball.

If the scratch marks are curved outwardly all the way from the front to the back edge of the sole, you are an out-and-out slicer. You may very well have been poorly fitted when you purchased your clubs. Your grip also may be faulty.

If the scratches start about halfway across the sole and curve toward the toe, you are tipping the face up and are not using *The Basic Movement*. If they start about halfway across the sole and curve toward the heel, you should have your club examined for accurate face alignment.

12. If the lacquer or varnish is worn off the center of the sole, you're doing fine. If there are no signs of wear in that area, you're either a slicer or you're scooping at the ball, and I suggest you see your golf doctor.

If there are visible signs of wear on the heel of your club, you have not acquired *The Basic Movement.*

13. If your hands are blistered or sore after playing, either your grip doesn't provide enough traction or you're holding the club too loosely.

14. If you cannot bring your club into true striking position with your eyes closed and the club off the ground, you should obtain an out-of-round grip—one that is flat or ridged on one side. Otherwise you have no way of checking the alignment of your club when you are making your swing.

15, 16. The answers to these questions give to the professional an indication of what your athletic tendencies are, and they help him to determine the type of game you play. If you move rapidly, walk rapidly, and talk rapidly, the indication is that you will probably swing rapidly and require a stiff shaft. If you are athletically inclined and have a strong body, you'll also require a stiff shaft. If you are a lighter or weaker individual, you will need a shaft with more whip. The chances are that those experienced in baseball and tennis will have little difficulty in learning balance.

Progress Tests

Here are a few simple tests you can give yourself from time to time to check whether you are correctly employing the basic golfing techniques.

1. Place three tees about one inch apart in your line of aim ahead of the ball. Make sure that the tees are of the same height as the tee holding your ball. Hit the ball. If you do not knock over the other tees, you are not swinging in the preferred flattened curve *(The Basic Movement).*

2. Place a ball on the ground. Place a book on edge, about eighteen inches from the ball and in the line of aim. Hit the ball with a 9 iron. If you knock the book over with the ball, you do not yet muscularly comprehend *The Basic Movement.* You may understand it mentally, but you're not using it.

3. Place two balls on the ground, perpendicular to your line of aim. Hit one, and compare the turf around it with the ground around the one you didn't hit. If you dug up turf before the ball, you'd better practice your *Basic Movement.* If you cut the turf after you made contact, you're doing fine.

4. Do you generally stub the turf on your short approach shots? If not, fine. If you do, it is further reason for you to practice *The Basic Movement.*

5. Hit a ball when it is on an inclined lie. Examine the ball. If you have cut the cover of the ball, it is a sure indication that you are not employing *The Basic Movement.*

6. Do you often hit the ball with the neck of the club? Do you *shank?* This word is evil. The very mention of it carries a fine in some circles. If you don't, keep reading. If you do, your balance is bad because your shoulders are too near the ground. Stand closer to the ball and raise the upper part of your body, in order to allow enough room for your club and arms to swing. Above all, allow your head to rotate with your swing. Don't be a turf gazer!

7. Place a yardstick on the ground. Select one spot, preferably in the middle, and bring your putter into true striking position. Take a backswing and return your putter to the spot you had selected. Did you return it to the same square position? If you did not, check the placement of your hands when you grip the putter. Try to line up the palms of your hands parallel to the face of your putter. If you do return your putter to its true striking position, you've no worry there.

4

Evolution of the Instruments . . . Clubs and Balls

A *HISTORY* of the clubs and balls is a history of the game. Since approximately the middle of the eighteenth century there have been three different kinds of balls: the feathery, made mostly of feathers with just a leather cover; the gutty, made of gutta percha; and the rubber-core, having a rubber-wound core with a gutta cover, subsequently made of balata. With certain refinements, the rubber-cored ball is the one most widely used today. As each of these balls appeared, it influenced the design of the clubs for its companion use.

The flight of the feathery ball was hard to control, owing to the smoothness of the painted leather cover. For that reason, the faces of the clubs—drivers, baffies, baffy spoons, and the like—were concaved between the heel and the toe. Cupping the faces made it easier for the player to control the ball. Since this kind of ball "got up" quite easily, the club faces had less loft than the clubs that appeared with the gutty ball, which succeeded the feathery in 1848.

The gutty, which was molded and made of one material throughout, was rounder than the entirely handmade feathery. Since its flight was truer, the club faces were changed from concave to straight.

There were other changes, of course. Important among them was fitting leather in the club faces. The gutty ball was comparatively hard and gave off quite a jar, especially when it wasn't hit squarely. Leather inserts in the club faces helped to absorb the shock.

Markings on the ball

When the gutty ball was first made, it had a smooth surface, and the players of the 1850's soon found that the ball got up and flew much better as the surface got roughened by play. So markings were deliberately applied, the earliest being those made with a cobbler's or shoemaker's hammer. Then the balls were marked by pass-

36

ing them through a trough against a corrugated wheel. It took three passes to obtain a complete pattern of markings around the ball.

The pattern of the semi-machine surface markings, unlike those of the hand-hammered variety, could be regulated for depth and frequency. As a result, the flight of a golf ball became a study in ballistics, and many designs of surface markings were developed. Emerging from the great variety were two patterns of proven superiority: the "square" and the "bramble." The square pattern had grooves with raised squares, and the bramble had raised semi-circular projections. Because the bramble performed better in all weather conditions, it became almost universally used up to, and shortly after, the arrival of the rubber-cored ball, which made its appearance around the turn of the century.

While these studies in ball flight were being evolved, there were players who preferred the square to the bramble and vice versa. The astute club-maker, in making clubs to order, would have to vary the club face lofts to suit the corresponding balls the player chose to use.

Changes in the club face

Club designers and makers were having a difficult time trying to keep pace with the rapid scientific advancement of the ball. It was only natural for the ball, as a projectile, to receive more attention than the clubs. A big step in the catching-up process was the invention of

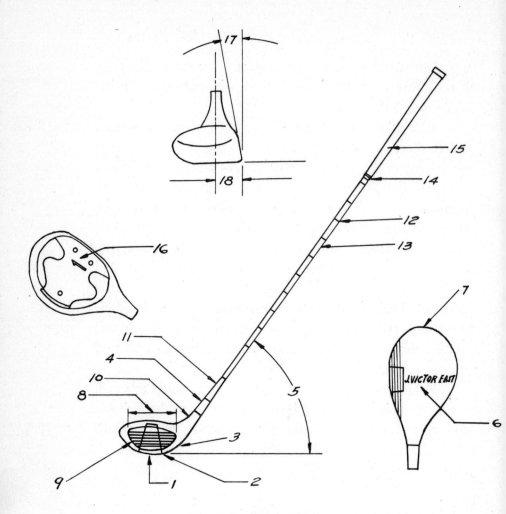

Identification of Parts
Woods

1.	Head	10.	Neck
2.	Sole	11.	Shaft Collar
3.	Heel	12.	Steps
4.	Neck Collar	13.	Shaft
5.	Lie	14.	Grip Trim
6.	Top Stamp	15.	Grip
7.	Nose	16.	Sole Plate
8.	Face	17.	Loft
9.	Corrugation	18.	Face Progression

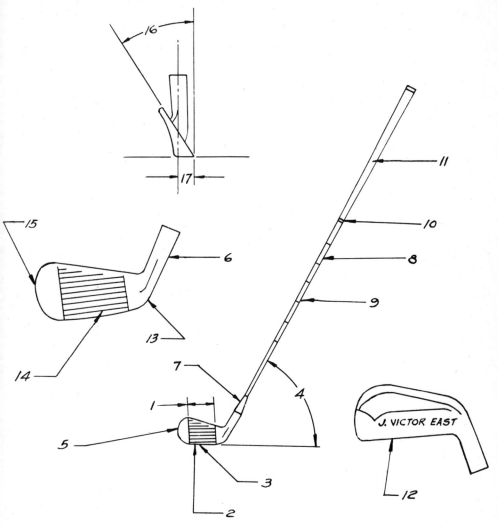

Identification of Parts
Irons

1. Face
2. Head
3. Sole
4. Lie
5. Blade
6. Hosel
7. Collar
8. Steps
9. Shaft
10. Grip trim

11. Grip
12. Back stamping
13. Heel
14. Corrugation
15. Toe
16. Loft
17. Face progression

How 1° Influences "Facing"

The tapered line shown above represents what would be a 1° change in club face angle. Note: A variation of 1° causes ball to change direction 30 to 40 feet in 225 yards of travel.

the bulger-faced club in 1895.

A British student of the game obtained a patent on his idea to build distance and direction into the club as well as the ball. He was probably influenced by the slightly convex face surface of the carpenter's hammer. This shape will drive nails truer and more accurately than a hammer with a flat surface, and this principle was incorporated into golf club design.

Since the uninformed golfer is apt to fear that the bulger-faced wood clubs require him to be more careful to meet the ball squarely, here follows some direct information concerning its influence on direction and distance.

Direction is the result of the angle and path of impact, or, to paraphrase it, "the ball goes where the club face looks." If the club face were flat and were to meet the ball squarely at a right angle to the line of intended direction, the ball would have to fly straight. As any golfer will testify, it is inhuman not to err. Should you stroke the ball at a glancing angle, with the heel ahead of the toe end, the result would be a slice to the right. Should that same shot be delivered from a club with a bulger face, the ball would be less off line, because the club face would be "looking" less to the right. The same would hold true if the ball were struck with the toe ahead of the heel. I call your attention to the diagrams that explain this.

Distance depends, primarily, on the energy built into the ball. The golf balls we use today are composed of rubber threads of high tensile strength wound over an inner resilient center. The deeper the penetration of the blow, the greater the intervening wound-rubber thread will stretch. The same applies to the deformation of the resilient inner center. The resulting snap-back, or reaction of both thread and center, is what adds to the ball's getaway.

This action and reaction of the ball under impact is commonly and quite erroneously described as "compression," for, as with fluids, rubber is not compressible, to my knowledge. People improve their stroke-making by comparing the high resiliency of the ball to the stretching of a high-quality rubber band. The speed of snap-back is in direct proportion to the amount of initial stretching. The realization that the ball changes shape under club im-

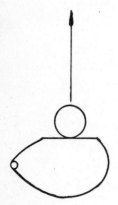 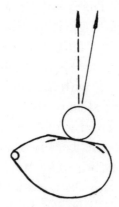 

With a flat face, a square impact would insure a straight flight.

Should the ball be struck with the heel ahead of the toe of a straight-faced club, the solid line would indicate the flight of the ball. The dotted lines indicate the correction the bulger face offers.

Should the ball be str with the toe ahead of heel, the ball would more to the left when str by the straight-faced c than it would with a bul faced club.

Note: *With every part of the human body in motion, a square impact with the club face and ball is quite difficult to achieve. This is why wood club faces are made with the corrective bulger face.*

pact, and reacts or reforms in the getaway, usually results in the application of maximum and sustained power both at and during contact with the ball.

The bulger face penetrates deeper into the heart of the golf ball than does the straight face. This extra stretch

42

out of the wound-rubber thread helps you to get greater distance. As true as this is, I offer a note of warning that applies to all but the very, very low-handicap players. Currently on the market are golf clubs with what is described as "roll" to the faces. This "roll" is an accentuated bulge in the vertical direction of the club face, not in the horizontal plane we have just discussed.

The danger of this roll face is that it is contrary to the first principles of the game, getting the ball into flight. There have been many changes in the equipment and the methods of play, but never has there been any change from the basic principle that the game is played, for the most part, from the ground via the air route to the objective. In fact, I can think of very few other ball games in which the ball is at ground level when struck. In most other games, the ball is hit from the air to the ground. The loft of the clubs, coupled with the proper execution of *The Basic Movement*, is what produces correct ball flight. The roll goes against the basic principles by decreasing loft and reducing the possibility of getting the ball up into a controlled flight, the real thrill in the game of golf. Stay away from clubs featuring the roll if you want to enjoy your game.

The influence of the rubber-cored ball

The entry of American efficiency and inventiveness into Ye Auld and Ancient Game of Golf was marked by the rubber-cored ball. This was indeed a history-making innovation. Somewhere near the turn of this century Doctor Haskell, an ardent follower of the game, conceived the idea that a golf ball could be improved greatly if it were to have a rubber winding with a protective covering. Such a ball came on the market, and, with quite a few refinements, is the ball in use today.

If memory serves me correctly, the ball's popularity stems from the success Walter J. Travis had with it in winning the British Amateur Championship. The golfers in Great Britain were so impressed with the results obtained by Travis with the Haskell rubber-cored ball that they paid one pound apiece (then equal to $4.80) for them.

Whether the doctor then knew it, or since came to know it, I don't know; but, having been in the golf business for over half a century, I can say that his invention was the greatest single contribution to the pleasure of playing golf. The solid gutty ball would thrill you when met squarely, but if you were to half-top it and repeat the topping a few times during the course of 18 holes, your finger joints would be stiff and sore the next day. What the balloon tire did for the comfort of motorists, the Haskell ball did for golfers.

The gutty was hard to get up, and the early Haskell ball was hard to keep down. Back in 1902 I was to play a money match against a fellow professional in Australia. He won the honor, teed up, and drove his ball into a pond far beyond what anyone had carried into before. His ball was not recovered. When we finished the game, he told me the ball he used off the first tee was one of those new rubber-cored Haskells, whereupon I confessed to him I had one, too, but because of its uncontrollability, I was too scared to spring it on him.

44

The very nature of this new ball called for the immediate redesign of all golf clubs, including even the putter. Since all golfers could not be supplied new clubs overnight, players with only "gutty ball clubs" had to compensate for the flightiness of the ball by changing their stroke. What subsequently became known as "pronation" in the swing came to be recognized as a way of controlling the flightiness of the new ball. But designs had to change to cope with the ball, and they appeared in this order: reduced club face lofts, stiffer shafts, thinner grips, deeper faces, hard face inserts instead of leather, redesign of head weight distribution, and changes in lies to a more "upright" swing.

As soon as club design caught up to the rubber-cored ball, the ruling authorities began to make changes. The golf ball was traveling too far, they said, and the courses were being outmoded. If this were to continue, more real estate would be required to lengthen the courses, and this would be far too expensive. As a result, the United States Golf Association started to set low limits on the size and high limits on the weight at which a ball could be made. The first of the limitations was a 1.620″ size and a 1.620 oz. weight. This was followed by a 1.680″ size and 1.550 oz. weight. The last change to a 1.680″ size and a 1.620 oz. weight brings us up to date.

As each decision to change the size and weight specifications were to become effective, the golf ball manufacturers were given advance notice to regulate inventories of balls and to get tooled up for the new ones. On the face of things, golfers had only a vague notion of what was happening to their individual games. All they knew was that not all balls performed alike. One change gave rise to player resentment, almost rebellion, against the USGA. This had to do with the switch from the 1.620″ and 1.620 oz. ball to the 1.680″ and 1.550 oz. ball. This ball, because it got up too high and was easily being blown off course, was nicknamed the "balloon ball." The players' objections, together with the bootlegging of the earlier 1.620″ and 1.620 oz. ball, gave the balloon ball but a short life.

Again, each ball change necessitated redesigning the controllable, result-getting characteristics of the clubs; and because Mr. and Mrs. Average Golfer had never been directly informed of the advantages of getting companion clubs for the different kind of balls, a large percentage battled along with clubs long since outmoded. Some people still use outmoded clubs.

The existing rules also restrict the initial velocity at which a ball may travel. The technicalities of the specifications require that the ball must be brought to a specific temperature when tested. The individual manufacturers have brought much scientific knowledge to bear in order to make their balls perform in accordance with the maximum allowed speed limits. From time to time the application of the scientific findings have changed the flight characteristics of the various makes of balls, which, in turn, automatically called for changes in clubs.

Suppose a manufacturer decides to change the surface markings on a ball. It may be a change in design, or a change of depth or frequency. It might lower the trajectory below the 70- to 80-foot peak-flight height the well-hit drive should reach. The user of such a ball can do one of two things: build more loft into his clubs, or use more flexible shafts in his distance clubs. The added flexibility due to the changed action and reaction when swung increases the club face loft. My advice to you is to get your professional to help you select the clubs to fit your individual physique. Then, by thoughtful testing, get the companion make of ball, and stay with the combination. Beyond this, always be alert for any change that may take place in the ball.

Points to Remember

- 1. Different types of balls affected changes in the design of clubs.

- 2. Stroke-making was affected by the design of clubs.

- 3. The rubber-cored ball was the greatest single contribution to the game of golf.

- 4. Changes in design of balls still dictate changes in design of clubs.

- 5. Be aware of any changes in golf ball design.

- 6. Try to stay with one combination of clubs and balls.

5

For a Firm Grip
on Your Game

7HE photographs of the changes in grips in the past one hundred years will show you how the different grips looked. But more important to us is why these changes took place. Club-makers did not vary the shape of grips in an effort to be different or unusual. Every change was an attempt to cope satisfactorily with a new problem resulting from a change in the ball, the club head, the shaft, or the method of stroke-making.

History of the grip

The first grip pictured represents those used fifty years ago and earlier. You'll notice that the grip was designed for the club that was used with the gutta percha ball. When this ball was struck, it gave off a shock; and the grip, much larger and heavier than those of today, was padded sufficiently to be shock absorbing.

The advent of the rubber-cored ball was the most important factor causing a reduction in grip size. No longer did the grip have to be thickly padded, like a shock absorber; and the wool fabric insulation could be removed. About this same time the overlapping grip, an entirely different method of grasping the club, became popular. The thumb of the upper hand remained on top of, rather than around, the grip. (See the illustration on page 57.) For the sake of comfort, the change called for a smaller grip size.

The upright swing influenced further reductions in grip size. The club was held less in the palm and came into the hands at a greater angle than had been the case with the earlier, flatter swing. This narrowed the channel that the grip formed within the hands, which necessitated the reduction in size. (This change to uprightness from what had previously been called the old St. Andrews swing has been carried on by most of the players of the newer generation—Bobby Jones, Tommy Armour, Byron Nelson, Sam Snead, Lloyd Mangrum, Tommy Bolt, and others.)

The switch from hickory shafts to steel shafts seriously complicated the problem of grip design. The steel

EVOLUTION
OF THE
GOLF CLUB GRIP
1850 • 1956

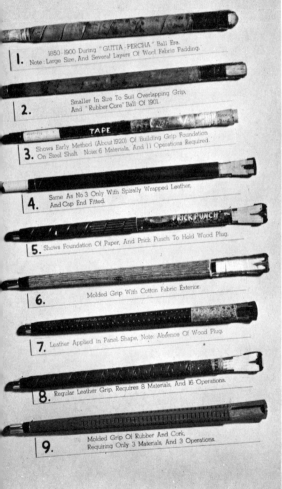

1. 1850-1900 During "GUTTA-PERCHA" Ball Era.
   Note: Large Size, And Several Layers Of Wool Fabric Padding.

2. Smaller In Size To Suit Overlapping Grip,
   And "Rubber Core" Ball Of 1901.

3. TAPE
   Shows Early Method (About 1920) Of Building Grip Foundation
   On Steel Shaft. Note: 6 Materials, And 11 Operations Required.

4. Same As No.3 Only With Spirally Wrapped Leather,
   And Cap End Fitted.

5. PRICK PUNCH
   Shows Foundation Of Paper, And Prick Punch To Hold Wood Plug.

6. Molded Grip With Cotton Fabric Exterior.

7. Leather Applied In Panel Shape, Note: Absence Of Wood Plug.

8. Regular Leather Grip, Requires 8 Materials, And 16 Operations.

9. Molded Grip Of Rubber And Cork,
   Requiring Only 3 Materials, And 3 Operations.

(1) *Wood shaft, with several layers of woolen cloth covered with sheepskin.*

(2) *Wood shaft, wrapped with a cotton fabric and covered with goatskin.*

(3) *Steel shaft, with a wood plug inserted in the end. It was then wrapped with friction tape, felt, a cotton fabric, and finally paper to blend the shape. It was spirally covered with calfskin.*

(4) *Same as (3), but with an end cap inserted in the wood plug.*

(5) *Steel shaft, with paper used for grip foundation.*
Note: *The wood plug was secured by prick punching through the steel shaft, which required annealing or drawing the temper from the steel shaft.*

(6) *Steel shaft, with a wood plug, a rubber-cork foundation, and a fabric covering.*

(7) *Steel shaft, with a rubber-cork foundation and kip leather applied in panel shape.*
Note: *This grip had no wood plug.*

(8) *Steel shaft, with a wood plug, a rubber-cork foundation, and fabric and paper to blend to shape. A plastic endcap was fastened with a screw and covered with calfskin tacked to the wood plug and finished off with plastic end cap.*

(9) *Steel shaft, with rubber-cork throughout and a unitary grip and cap molded in one operation.*

shaft gave off quite a sharp sting whenever the golfer struck the ball the slightest amount off center. It is safe to say that if it had not been for the presence of the rubber-cored ball with its shock-absorbing qualities, steel shafts would never have become popular. The steel shafts, however, could be made stronger and lighter than the old hickory shafts; and these qualities insured that steel shafts were here to stay. Just how to get away from "the sting of steel" was quite a problem for club engineers and designers. To give you some idea of the research job it involved, I shall list the objectives I originally set up in 1932, along with comments on subsequent developments.

Specifications of the future golf club grip

(The prime requirement was that the future grip be "grippable" for all types of hands and for all climates. This could be accomplished by satisfying the following:)

1. *Must not hurt hands or blister skin.* Rubber had previously been used, but rubber alone caused blisters because it prevented traction. The blister problem was solved by a substance providing more adhesion and constancy of traction.
2. *Must absorb perspiration.* Neither rubber nor leather absorbs perspiration. Cork in combination with rubber satisfied this requirement.
3. *Must disperse perspiration.* In the same way an automobile tire provides traction by dispersing water on wet pavements, the golf club must disperse perspiration. This was solved by making recesses in the rubber pattern.

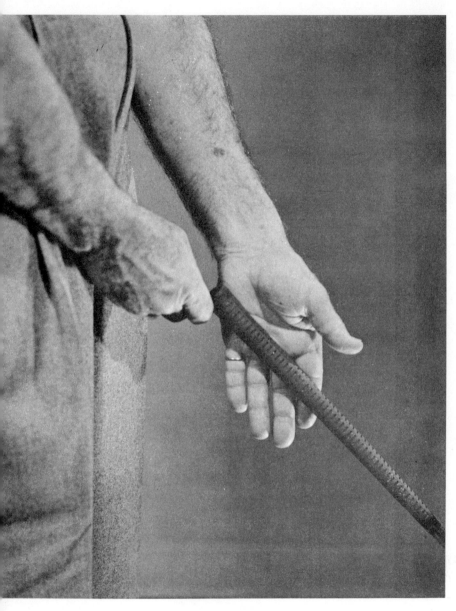

How to Grip

(1) The club poised diagonally alongside the left hand.

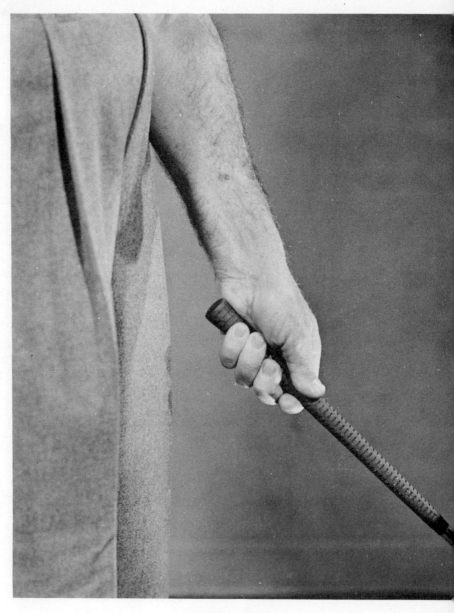

How to Grip

(2) The left hand closed.

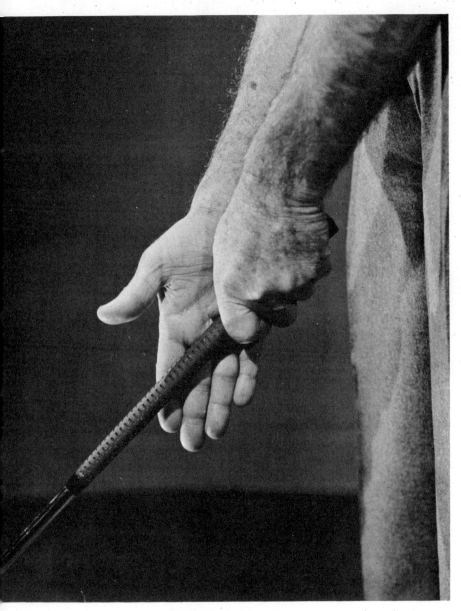

How to Grip

(3) The right hand alongside.

Note: *The club comes more across the fingers than*
when gripped with the left hand, as in (1).   55

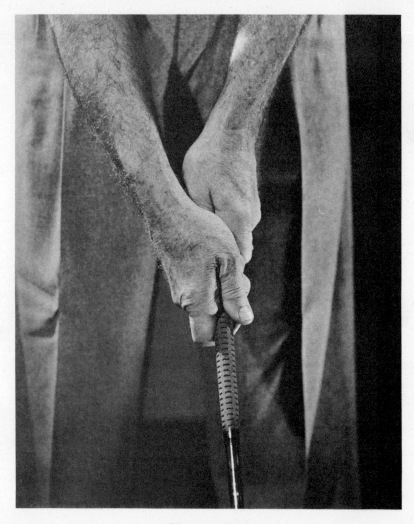

How to Grip

(4) The right hand closed, with the thumb of the left hand snugly fitted in the groove of the right palm.

Note: *The hooked knuckle of the right index finger extends beyond the thumb. Also, as shown here and as will be seen in the pictures entitled* How to Aim, *the V's formed by the closed thumb forks of both hands do not point between the head and right shoulder. This differs from the lineup of the V's more commonly advocated, but is consistent with the grip technique of the present-day leading players.*

HOW TO GRIP

(5) Underside view of the overlapping grip.

Note: *The little finger of the right hand crosses diagonally the second knuckle of the right index finger. This is an important detail. Placement of the little finger should be the* last *step.*

HOW TO GRIP

(6) Underside view of the interlocking grip.

4. *Must absorb shock.* When you send a ball traveling at 100 m.p.h., the original impetus that sends it at such speed must cause a certain amount of shock. Although cotton, wool, and other paddings had been tried, the inherent qualities of rubber provided the solution. One of the most important properties of rubber compounds is their ability to store large amounts of energy. This energy-storing ability is approximately 150 times greater than that of spring-tempered steel. It is this property that makes rubber so ideal to absorb shock and dampen vibration.

5. *Must have traction.* To permit you to get a firm grip and maintain control of the club, recesses were provided to act like the treads on a tire.

6. *Must be slip proof.* To prevent your hands from slipping up and down the shaft, indentations in the grip were included.

7. *Must not allow twisting.* To prevent the club face from rotating because of the circular twisting of the club, an out-of-roundness was developed. This assures the golfer that his club face is square, even when he is swinging.

8. *Must reduce grip-joint tension.* When you don't have to grip so tight to maintain control of the club, you enjoy greater freedom of movement in the hands and wrists. The energy previously used to control the club can be transferred to an increased club-head speed. All the aforementioned developments aided in this respect.

9. *Must be lightweight.* If you reduce the weight of the grip, as you do with a rubber-cork compound, you lower the overall club weight. All other weights being constant, you are then lowering the center of gravity. This causes an increased swing weight, which provides more force at the moment of impact.

10. *Must be uniform in weight and size.* This uniformity obviates the necessity of assuming a different posture as you go from club to club.

11. *Must provide variety—shapes, sizes, colors.* As much as this is an age of speed, it is also an age of color. Individual tastes and requirements were satisfied.

12. *Must have a neat appearance.* No animal hides are ever completely uniform. This is a quality that can be achieved only through the use of synthetic materials.

13. *Must be easy to apply and service.*

14. *Must be durable.*

15. *Must be lower in price than the present grips.*

The last grip shown in the accompanying photograph of the grip changes through the past half-century complies with the above specifications.

Thorn sticks and Harry Vardon come to grips

With few exceptions, most golfers, both champions and duffers, employ the overlapping grip, popularized by the great British champion, Harry Vardon. I asked him

how he came to use this grip, and this is what he told
me.

> Where I lived as a boy, there were lots of
> black thorn sticks around, and we used to swing
> with them. I found that if I put my thumb on
> the stick and not around it, the way the golfers
> did, I didn't get pricked with the thorns. As a
> result, the little finger on my right hand started
> riding over the first knuckle of my left. When
> I later got a chance to hit a ball with a regular
> club, I tried to do as the others did, with the
> thumbs around the shaft. I couldn't control the
> ball so well, so I reverted back to my old thorn
> stick method.

And so the grip on the golf club was revolutionized.
Ben Hogan, Sam Snead, and Bobby Jones favor the overlapping grip, while Gene Sarazen and Francis Ouimet
achieved their success with the interlocking grip. Lloyd
Mangrum uses a variation of the interlocking grip. He,
unlike Gene and Francis, places his left thumb on the shaft,
nicely fitted in the groove formed between the thumb and
palm of the right hand.

Which grip shall I use?

Obviously then, there isn't just one way to grip the
club. I might point out that there have been four successful grips: the palm, the thumb and finger, the overlapping, and the interlocking. Regardless of differences
in detail, all have been alike in respect to the one essential

requirement that the palms of the hands line up with the club face. I shall discuss this more completely later in this chapter. As far as your individual grip is concerned, that will depend on your size, your strength, your preference, and probably the golfing hero you most desire to emulate.

The blindfold test

The golf club grip has been round for about five hundred years, but it had always been my contention that it could be improved upon. My reasons were:
(1) You cannot tell by feel alone the direction of the club face. You have to look at it.
(2) You must exert too much strength to prevent the club from twisting and slipping while you are swinging it.
(3) By exerting extra effort to get a firm grip on the club, you restrict the free movements of the finger and wrist joints. This causes your club head to lose speed, and you lose your sensitive control over the angle of the club face.

When you swing a club with a round grip, you must see as well as feel where the club face lies. This was proven in a most conclusive manner at a meeting where the subject was discussed with twelve nationally-known golfers.

Each had been asked to bring along one of his own wooden clubs. Each, in turn, was requested to close his eyes, and was handed his own club. Then he was further requested to bring the club face around to its square or true striking position, with the club held approximately

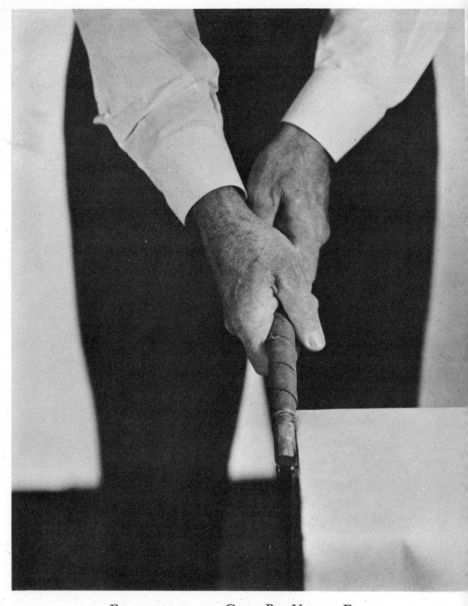

Evolution of the Grip—Pre-Vardon Era

(1) Note the large size of the grip and the angle at which it comes across the hand.

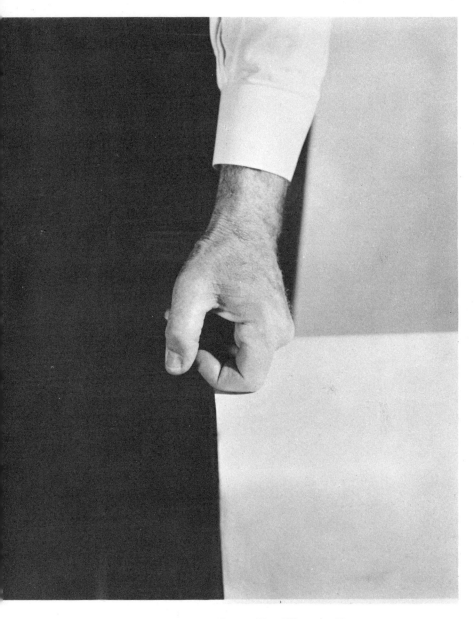

EVOLUTION OF THE GRIP—PRE-VARDON ERA

(2) Note how large the opening had to be to grip this type of club.

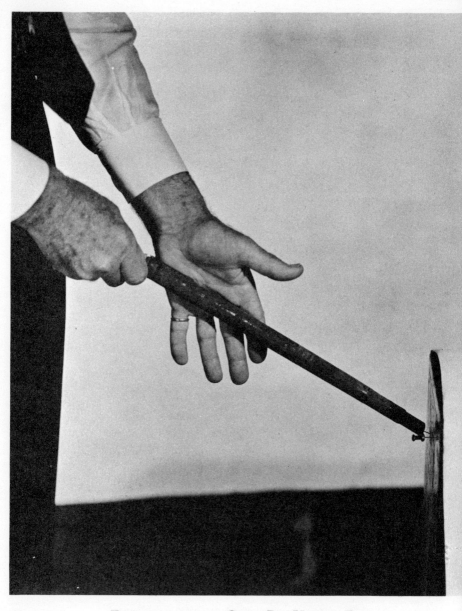

EVOLUTION OF THE GRIP—PRE-VARDON ERA

(3) The grip that was considered correct up to about 1900. It was used at that time as commonly as the overlapping grip is used today.

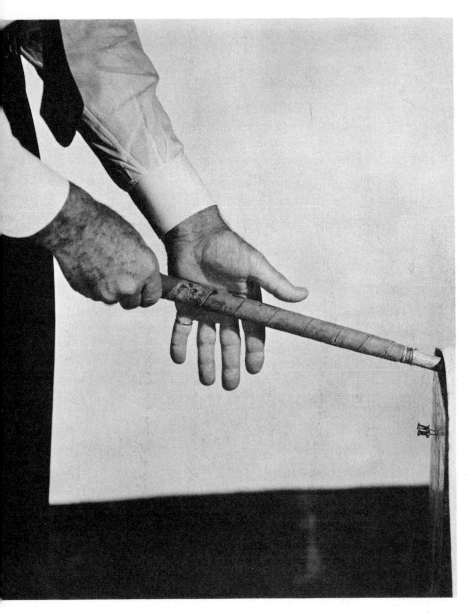

EVOLUTION OF THE GRIP—AFTER VARDON

*(1) The club comes more diagonally into the hand
than it did with the earlier grip.*

EVOLUTION OF THE GRIP—AFTER VARDON

(2) Note the smaller channel to receive the club.

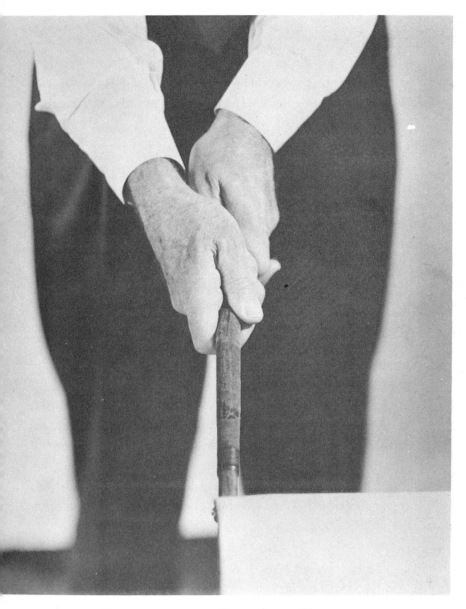

EVOLUTION OF THE GRIP—AFTER VARDON

(3) To compare the notable difference between the new and the old ways of gripping, note the closed V's between the thumbs and index fingers in this picture and the open V's in the picture on page 64.

six inches from the floor. Of the twelve, only one got the club face properly lined up; and he, a former U. S. Open Champion, could not do it again in six more attempts. A former winner of the Los Angeles Open Tournament was chagrined when he opened his eyes and saw his club face looking at the ceiling.

Having what might aptly be called the blindfold test in mind, I suggest to anyone who reads this book that, if his clubs have round-shaped grips, he might well try this experiment. If, like these nationally-known players, he fails to find the face by feel, he will improve his play by using modern clubs with shaped grips.

You will be interested to know that many of today's leading players, including some recent open champions, use clubs having under-ribs or ridges. All the shaped grip does is to simplify, to lessen another bugaboo. The grip tells the golfer that the club face is properly lined up as an extension of his hands while the club is in motion. He can't look at it to check its position in the middle of a swing. This out-of-round grip enables the golfer to tell that the club face is in a proper striking position by his sense of feel alone. If the grip has a ridge on it, you are informed and have good control—if it is round, you have no means of control.

The face of the club should be an extension of the hands

You can concentrate on only one thing during your golf stroke. Right now your full concentration should

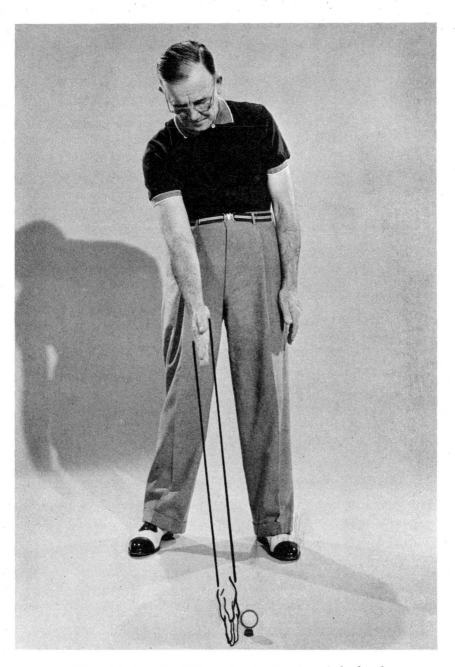

The club face should be a direct extension of the hand.

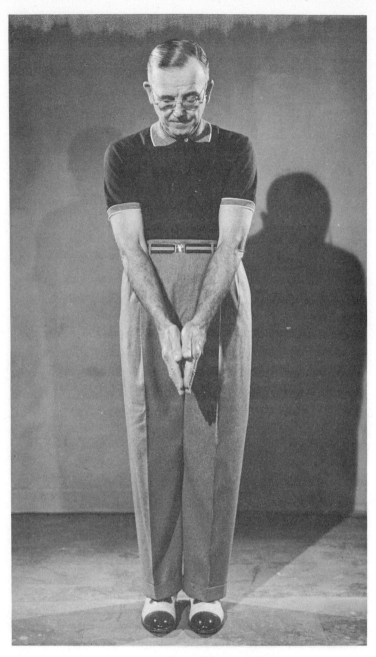

Holding the palms together.

70

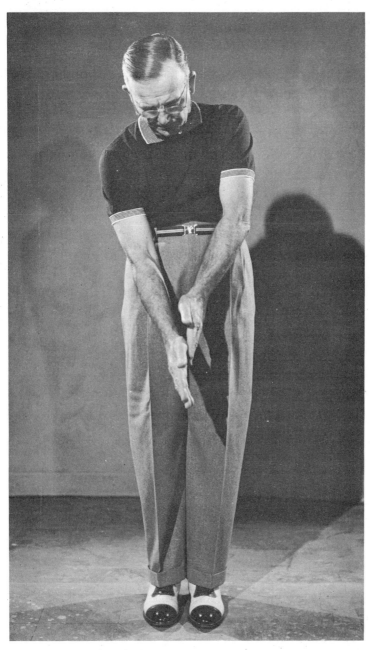

Sliding the right hand down and the left hand up.
Note the tilt of the head and shoulders.

71

be on *The Basic Movement*, and it should remain there until you can execute *The Basic Movement* without thinking about it. Eventually, your attention will center on the ball itself; but this is a discussion I shall save until later.

To execute *The Basic Movement* most effectively, the face of the club should be thought of as an extension of your two hands. Imagine yourself, for a moment, standing over a golf ball without a club in your hands. If your arm were long enough to reach the ball from that position, you'd find that the easiest and most natural way to strike the ball would be with the palm of your right (or left) hand.

It is for this reason that I stress the importance of lining up the palms with the face side of the club. When you close your hands in this position, you not only produce a correct grip, but also, with a slight bending of your knees, insure comfortable balance. Follow these simple steps:

    (1) With your eyes looking down at the ball, bring your palms together.

    (2) Your left hand goes up the shaft, your right hand down the shaft (reverse for left-handers).

    (3) Close your hands on the club.

Now it's up to you to do what you wish with your fingers. Using whichever grip you prefer, you will find that the face of the club has become an extension of your hands (particularly the palm side of your lower hand).

When teaching, I used a cutaway club like the one in the photograph. I found it of considerable help when I was explaining to a pupil how to grasp the club. He would then be able to accept more readily the concept that the club was a true extension of the hands. It was also my experience that, when a pupil understood that a golf club should be gripped with both hands acting as a single unit, and was then given a cutaway club to practice with, he readily overcame the bad habit of getting his hands out of proper gripping position. Actually, a common yardstick can be used to accomplish the same thing.

Balance for power

A sound, correct grip is a vital factor in developing balance without conscious effort. Observe the good professional golfer when he swings. Every ounce of energy he can summon is exploded at the moment of impact, when the face of the club strikes the ball. He ends as he began, in perfect balance.

The hapless duffer—and there might be one or two in my audience—has a tendency to fall backwards or forwards when he swings at the ball with all his power. In ninety-nine cases out of a hundred, his trouble comes from a faulty grip. Any effort to compensate for a poor hold on the club will be transferred unequally to the feet, and will tip you off balance. Once your balance is thrown

This cutaway club shows the relationship of the palms
of the hands to what would ordinarily be the club face.

The cutaway club showing the flatness of the grip to flatness of the face.

75

off, you know that somewhere there is wasted effort that should be harnessed to produce club head speed. Select a grip with the aid of your club professional. Practice that grip until it becomes habit and your balance will come naturally.

Keep your movements natural

Since the average person has no trouble with his sense of balance, the logical thing to do is to depart from your walking or standing posture only as much as it is absolutely necessary to grip a golf club. Get a comfortable stance. Lean forward just far enough to bring your palms together on the club. And lean sideways no more than to allow the palms to be separated by the length of one hand. If you get into this position and then look where the ball is to be placed, you should be able to grip the club without any strain.

Points to Remember

- 1. Place feet apart, about shoulder width.

- 2. Look where ball would be placed.

- 3. Bring palms of hands together.

- 4. Place club between hands.

- 5. Slide one hand *up*, the other *down*.

- 6. Close hands without changing club or body position.

- 7. Never look at hands. Get grip by "feel" alone.

- 8. Practice until correct grip has become habit.

6

How to Take Aim
for Best Results

THE club head has progressed from a crude wooden knob to a synthetic, precision-manufactured product of chemistry and engineering, accurate to within one fourth the width of a human hair. Although correct aiming in golf is a procedure that depends largely on the execution of certain physical and mental habits, the results you obtain depend on the tools you use. New ideas have changed golf club design, and each change has helped us move closer to perfection. The proof is in our lower scores. The average winning scores in the British Open for three 25-year periods and in the American Open for two 25-year periods show that in both cases the winning average has been cropped five full strokes for each quarter-century. I attribute this to the common acceptance of (1) the rubber-cored ball and (2) the steel shaft. I also predict that, as new materials become commonly accepted, a similar reduction in average scores will result.

History of the club head

With the advent of the gutty ball, the club head began to develop rapidly toward the precision instrument it is today. The shape of the face changed from concave to straight, as mentioned earlier. The length of the head was contracted, and the depth of the face was increased slightly. Club-makers put leather inserts, usually of buffalo hide, into the club faces to absorb some of the shock given off by the solid gutta percha ball. English beech was the standard material used in carving the club heads.

In those early gutty days, club-makers did most of the work by hand. The block for the head was a knee-shaped piece of wood, on which the club-maker penciled his pattern. He worked this knee block down to the required size and shape with a hand band saw, a smaller fret saw, and then rasps and files. Once he established the shape, he fitted a piece of ram's horn for sole protection and inserted lead for weight. Although some new clubs were made with the leather faces already fitted, the more common practice was to use the club for a period of time and then fit the leather face.

It was in the mid-gutty days that club-makers brought the turning lathe into use. The machine age had arrived in club-making, and the old club-makers who are still around will recall the great saving of energy that the introduction of the "turned head" meant. The old sawed blocks became a thing of the past; and the band and fret saws were put away. There was still a considerable amount of hand labor performed, however, when you compare the methods of then and now. The bulger face became popular about this time; and the size of the head was further reduced in all proportions except in depth.

After 1901, to meet the problem of keeping the new rubber-cored ball down, club-makers reduced the lofts of the club faces. Harder materials replaced the leather faces—fiber, horn, metal, and other materials were used. With each redesign of the rubber-cored ball, the design of the club head had to keep pace.

The difference between conventional and modern clubs

Not too long ago, I suggested eliminating wood and forged steel as materials that were too inaccurate to be used in golf clubs. The average, present-day club head picks up enough moisture to distort it in size, weight, and shape, not only when it is wet, but even more so when it is dried out. Face insets and sole plates fitted in wood add further inaccuracies. The most up-to-date clubs are made of synthetics impervious to moisture and changes in climate, and can be built to the most exact measurements. These materials very closely resemble wood in weight, tone quality, and feel. Even the familiar sound of the solid crack of a wood club against a ball has been duplicated.

I also insisted that the forging process was too inaccurate to maintain close tolerances. In a forging it was found that the location of the center line of the shaft and the face of the club was off by as much as $\frac{1}{32}$ of an inch (enough to throw the ball a hundred feet off line on a 225-yard shot). Newer, more accurate processes have been developed by club manufacturers who have kept pace with the times.

Machine tests have shown that the old-style club, because of the moisture pickup of the woods and the inherent inaccuracies of the forged irons, varied from one to four degrees, resulting in a difference of forty to one hundred and sixty feet on a 225-yard drive. More up-to-date clubs are accurate to within one half of one degree.

The conventional club is made of either American persimmon or laminated plywood; but both materials have a number of disadvantages. The club heads are impossible to control for true precision manufacturing; are vulnerable to moisture; and will chip, crack, and change shape. Most recently developed materials have been proven to be far stronger and more impervious to moisture than wood, and are of such composition as to lend themselves completely to true precision manufacturing.

The conventional club head is formed by turning the wood block on a lathe to the approximate size and shape required and then sanding by eye. (No two sanders will produce the same shape.) The impossibility of attaining true accuracy in such a process is evident. In fact, exhaustive tests of some of the finest clubs made indicated that face surfaces were off a minimum of one degree. The majority were considerably higher. *One degree of distortion can throw the direction of the ball off forty feet in a 225-yard shot.* (This was proved by actual test.)

The most modern manufacturing processes can produce clubs to an accuracy of .001 of an inch.

Moisture is the greatest scourge to all wooden clubs, both persimmon and laminated. In fact, a wood can pick up enough moisture on a dewy fairway to affect the swing weight by as much as one to three points . . . and distort the face several degrees. Also, once a wood has changed its shape as a result of moisture, it never returns to its original shape. As a point of interest, the swing weight of a wood club can change as much as five to ten points from one part of the country to another. With the latest of synthetic materials from which club heads are now being made, the golfer has no such problem.

The face insert of a wood is always made of a material other than wood, either plastic, fiber, or the like. Each material has a different moisture coefficient than wood. Thus the swelling of the wood caused by moisture makes it pull away from the insert and/or change its position. This is why you will frequently find that the insert on your club slightly protrudes or recedes from the face, or that there is a decided gap between the insert and the wood. The effect of this distortion on the accuracy of your shot is obvious.

In the clubs of today, the insert is of the same material as the head, and is fused to the head mechanically, chemically, and thermally. Further, the need for screws is eliminated, thus removing another common cause of distortion of the face insert on the conventional club.

This gives you a brief idea of some of the things club manufacturers and designers are doing to increase the accuracy of your club head. If you are properly tooled for the task, half the battle is won. The clubs won't aim themselves, however, so now I offer you the other half— a few suggestions on the most practical manner to give direction to your shots.

What are we aiming for?

You take aim between the time you approach the ball and begin your "waggle," or preliminary swing. This is the point at which your mastery of the grip and proper execution of *The Basic Movement* become most important. For once you start on your swing, you pass control of your club from your combined senses of sight and feel to habit. There is no longer time for any last-second adjustments. If your grip and *Basic Movement* do not flow naturally as the result of habit, the time you take to aim might just as well be spent on wishing.

You can master these fundamentals only through practice. With regards to your grip, I suggest keeping a club handy. Pick it up and get into your correct grip at frequent intervals until it becomes routine. Cultivate the feel of where the sole of the club is actually located when you are swinging. In the event your handicap is ten or more, you should confine exercise at first to not more than a half-swing, with the object of testing how well you can brush the sole of your club along a floor or other level surface. You should continue this exercise until you no longer bump the surface with either the front or back edge of your club sole. Then extend your exercise to a full swing.

For a revealing and convincing test, I suggest you swing your club sole across a gravel or concrete surface, since the resulting scratches will assist in cultivating the correct feel of knowing what is exactly right. The bottom edge of the club is your sight for aiming, and it must go through *in line with and square to* the direction you want. It is by feel only that you can expect to make proper contact with the ball.

The duffer takes aim

The other day I happened to notice a young fellow about fifty yards from the green on the third hole. He walked up to where his ball lay and began to position his feet. He kept his head down and glanced toward the hole out of the corner of his eye. After grasping and regrasping his club several times, he went into his waggle. He stopped, tucked in his right elbow, and then started again. It was a relatively cool day; but he stepped back, tucked his club under his arm, and began to mop his neck and hands with his handkerchief. Then he stepped up to the ball and started his waggle again. Then he stopped. He sneaked a look at the hole. He very deliberately gripped the club and took one deep, quite audible sigh.

I walked over to him, thinking I could offer some assistance.

"Excuse me," I said, "may I . . ."

"Stand back. Stand back, please. Can't you see I'm taking aim?"

With slight variations here and there, most duffers follow some similar set of gyrations when going through their aiming process. You will find that it will be a lot easier if you would standardize your aiming procedure. Try to follow this same pattern each time you prepare to make a shot.

(1) *Place the club* (properly gripped) to the ball in the position in which you want it to make contact during *The Basic Movement.*

(2) *Look at the objective.* Rotate, do not lift, the head in sighting.

(3) *Your left foot and club face* will automatically take position to insure the angle of play. The right foot adjusts itself in relation to the left.

85

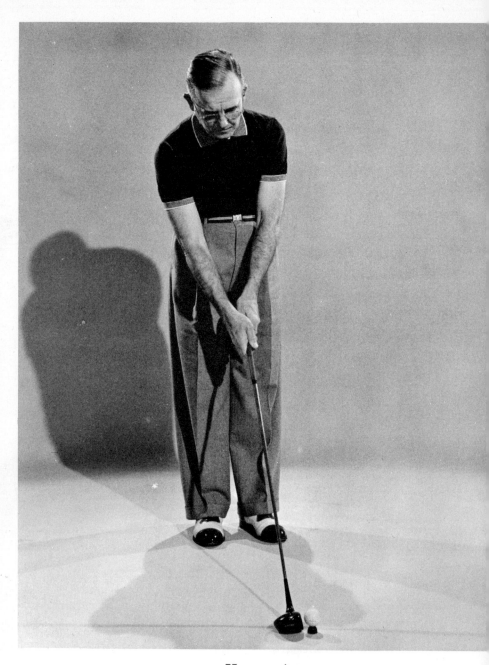

How to Aim

(1) Holding the club to the ball.

How to Aim

*(2) Placing the eyes on the objective and the club
to the angle of aim, with the left foot positioned.*

87

HOW TO AIM

(3) The right foot adjusted.

How to Aim

) *The* right *way to look at the objective.*

(5) *The* wrong *way to look at the objective.*

Note: *Fortunately, those who look around to the objective as in (5) are few and far between. For as the eyes look so do the hands strike; and looking around in this manner usually results in one smothered shot after another, unhappily for both pupil and teacher.*

A champion takes aim

Of the champions of this past half-century, the most efficient in taking aim and having the preliminaries of the address flow smoothly into their respective swings are Bobby Jones and Gene Sarazen. Each has that special brand of artistry that enables him to take aim without any apparent effort and within a minimum of time. Other players have taken less time, but their doing so might be described as hasty indecision rather than precision, seriously handicapping their chances of attaining real or enduring greatness.

Taking a tee shot, for example, Bob Jones, having arrived at the pattern of stroke to be played, would approach the ball from the left, rear side. He would casually place the forward side of his club face alongside the ball. He would then look from the ball along the line of play. Meanwhile, as he moved around with his club, his left foot—and at the same time—his club face—would line up squarely with the intended ball direction as a matter of habit. With his club and left foot oriented, Bob, in continued smooth progression, would start his preliminary waggle. During this time, his right foot would become adjusted by turning slightly outward from its original position, in which it pointed toward the ball. The waggle would be over when the club momentarily returned to the ball; and he'd move right into his backswing.

The point I want to emphasize is that this great champion of yesteryear, having once decided on the kind of shot to be played, maintained mobility until the ball got underway. He remained in motion while taking aim, addressing the ball, and making his stroke. Each movement progressed so smoothly into the next that they blended into one complete whole. Hence it is that Gene Sarazen, in his recently published book, so aptly described the golf stroke as the "one-piece swing." Of the present-day players, Sam Snead is the best exponent of the smooth stroke-making technique just described.

Let's get some light on the subject

So often golfers are led to believe that misdirection of the ball is due to an error in swing. One student of mine was convinced that his error was in his swing. My contention was that he did not aim properly beforehand; and anything he did, consciously or otherwise, to compensate for the basic error was unsound practice. He was so insistent I decided on a way to prove how he was wrong. I had a small electric bulb set squarely in the face of a wood club and connected it with a wire up through the shaft to a battery. The light would flash in the direction you would aim. In a semi-darkened room, I proved to his complete satisfaction that his pre-aiming in the direction in which he expected the ball to go was far off line. I call your attention to the pictures of this aim-testing device on the accompanying pages.

I am not suggesting that you construct a similar device; it would be too expensive. However, I do suggest that in practicing your aim you use a wood club rather

How to Aim

(6) Note the wire running from the top of the club to a battery in the left pocket. Pressure from the left hand on the battery readily flashes a light in the club face, showing whether the aim is on or off the target. The inset picture shows the light bulb and reflector.

than an iron. The wider sole of the wood makes more definite the proper placing of the sole.

Points to Remember

- 1. Sole the club squarely.

- 2. Grip the club before placing it to the ball.

- 3. Walk toward and place club to ball.

- 4. Look at objective by rotating, not lifting, head.

- 5. Feel when shaft and club face are square to objective.

- 6. Do not be foot conscious.

- 7. Move club back and forth behind ball. *Feel* and *see* that the club face is moving in a suitable path along the line of direction.

7

How to Put Sing
into Your Swing

*I*N the days of the feathery-centered and leather-cased balls, golf club sets contained more wood clubs than irons. In fact, it was not until about the time of the gutta percha ball that "iron" clubs were counted as a part of the player's equipment. The earliest of the irons was the track iron, subsequently called the niblick. This was followed by the lofter, the cleek, the medium iron, the mashie, the mashie niblick, and numerous others.

History of the shaft

The shafts were of a mixed variety, but American hickory readily proved superior to all others. What was commonly known as lemonwood was the last to go, prior to the acceptance of hickory. The shafts used with the gutty ball were of the whippy or supple variety; and the grips were quite thick, with soft leather applied. This extra padding was necessary to accommodate the grip (The overlapping and interlocking grips were not common.) and to provide the player with the required quality of "feel." Nowadays with the use of inorganic materials for making golf clubs the quality of feel is measurable and controllable to any degree.

With the advent of the bulger faces, the attachment between the shaft and the club head changed. Up to this time the head had been attached to the shaft by splicing and gluing the two parts, whipping being used to help maintain the bond. Because of its susceptibility to changing weather conditions, splicing had to give way to socketing. When Walter Hagen won his last British Open Championship, he used a *spliced* hickory-shafted driver.

The drilled or socketed type was a definite advance. Not only did it contribute to the more compact design of the head, but it also reduced the chances of heads coming off or, as it was called at the time, "coming loose in the glue," in the course of play. With the drilled construction, the shaft was fitted into the head. And so, when glued, the joint was better protected against the weather and lasted longer.

The rubber-cored ball, with its shock-absorbing properties, made the steel shaft a possibility; for had the solid gutty ball continued to be used, the sting given off by the steel would have been accented. In any case, the steel shafts were confined almost entirely to wood-headed clubs in the early stages. Initial attempts to use them in the irons were without success.

The modern shaft

The principal contributions of the more recent years have undoubtedly been the correctly matched sets and the general application of steel shafts to all clubs. The matched set idea covers a lot of territory. In both woods and irons, the principal considerations were: even increments of lies and lofts, uniform lengths and heights of heads, more uniform location of points of percussion, a uniform relationship between head and shaft weights, uniformity of shaft deflections, uniform shaft torsion, and lengths of clubs more nearly related to lies. And, finally, although there were many other considerations, the most important was a closer uniformity of swing weights in matched sets.

The modern shafts are the most closely weight-controlled golf shafts ever produced, which enables them to flex more uniformly and have more consistency of feel to the golfer. This means the golfer can take the same individual swing with every club within his set and expect optimum results from each shot—the only difference being that, as the lofts increase, the ball will rise higher. No intuitive compensations need be made for the equipment. This equipment promotes good form by allowing the golfer to concentrate on one swing.

Newer, stronger alloys are improving the steel shafts. This permits manufacturers to lighten the hosel and thus bring the impact point of each club nearer to its geometrical center. This also permits the lowering of the center of gravity, which results in increased swing weight in relation to the total weight of the clubs—thus greater distance can be obtained with the same effort.

Lest we forget . . .

Your improvement in golf is dependent on your proper execution of *The Basic Movement*. As strong as your grip, as perfect as your aim, as graceful as your swing may be, they will all go for naught unless you employ *The Basic Movement* in each shot you take. You have all seen, at one time or another, the little man outdrive the bigger man on the course or driving range. You have also seen some beautiful swings which produce nothing. Keep in mind throughout this chapter that the swing is only the means of executing *The Basic Movement*. If you have not yet mastered *The Basic Movement*, proceed with caution.

The waggle is part of the swing

Most books on golf, at least nearly all I have read this past half-century, describe the swing as what takes place after the waggle is over. Normally, the swing would be described to you as what happens, or should happen, from the time the club leaves the ball in the backswing. I think the swing starts quite a bit sooner. Earlier, I told how Bob Jones and Gene Sarazen use their address or preliminary waggle to get their respective swings organized and underway. I shall go even further and state that the swing actually gets started the instant the mental decision is made on the type of shot to be played.

I can imagine a beginner thinking, "That leaves me out." He is not even sure he's going to hit the ball, let alone having any catalogue to draw from on the type of shot to be played. In such a case, I would emphasize that the swing must flow from the moment you initially place the club face to the ball. To have this come about, you should thoroughly understand what is to take place in the preliminary waggle.

You want to hit the ball in a given direction. At no time should you do anything to cause a separation between your senses of sight and feel. Having obtained a correct grip on the club, and having handled the club enough to know the face side is to act as an extension of your hands, you should then focus your attention on the ball. This forces you to look at the ball and, then, on where the ball is to go. Your eyes, in combination with your sense of feel, should register proper aim. Your address should be a preliminary testing of whether, from your position, you can make a square impact with the ball. Reassured by these preliminaries, you should continue the original motion smoothly into that of the backswing. Your movement is slowed down, not noticeably stopped, when you return the club to, and "through," the ball and complete the swing.

Having a proper sequence helps you to produce a smooth swing in good tempo. Just whether the sequence contains more than one address or test waggle is a matter of individual mental assurance and composure. However, this much is certain: If, from the moment a person walks up to the ball, he indulges in any aimless handling of the club or breaks his proper sequence, the chances of his ever getting a good swing become so diminished as to condemn him to dufferdom forever.

Preparation for your swing

I don't want you to get the idea that this sequence is hastily carried out. A look at what the accomplished player must do in preparing to swing would be helpful:

(1) *Select the club.* As you walk to your ball, you will get a fairly general idea of the club required for the distance. You will arrive at the actual decision only after you take a close look at how the ball is lying. Should it be an unexpected lie, you might have to use a different club.

99

(2) *Place the club to the ball.*

(3) *Focus on the objective.*

(4) *Register aim.*

(5) *Waggle.* This confirms by seeing and feeling that your position is comfortable and right. If you regularly use the "forward press," this is the time for it. If you don't use the forward press, forget about it—it would just be something else to confuse you at this point.

(6) *Continue the stroke into the back swing.* The back swing is never initiated by a separate action.

While some good golfers are more deliberate than others, none is so immobile as to come to an actual dead stop anywhere in the sequence of movement. Seldom will you see the better players make any movement with the club in the address or waggle unless they feel and know that that movement actually fits in with sending the ball along the intended line of flight.

The natural result—the swing

The swing itself is the process of making a natural stroke with a club at a ball located in a stationary position. The development of your swing will come along quite naturally after you have obtained your correct grip and aiming procedure; and you follow these by getting the

How to Swing

(1) The forward press.

101

club started off in a suitable path of action—*The Basic Movement*. Actually, the effective swinging of a golf club is little different from what anyone would do if, instead of hitting a ball, he had merely to decapitate dandelions or clover blossoms.

Anytime I think of the swing as a natural process, I am reminded of my two native friends on Pago Pago. Joe Kirkwood and I met them during a brief layover on our tour of the South Pacific. Trying to get some exercise while the steamer was in port, Joe was hitting some balls with a 1 iron. A young native, about twenty years old, picked up a 2 iron after he had watched Joe hit a few. I was curious to see what he could do, so I encouraged him to take a try. Although he didn't fare too well on his first swing, his second shot was a solid hit that sent the ball as far as Joe's were carrying with his 1 iron. His next five swings produced similar results. My only advice to him was to hold the club so it would not be inclined into the ground and possibly break. With this one adjustment, his swings at the ball would have done justice to a scratch player.

Our other friend, a twelve-year-old boy, wasn't playing golf at all; but it certainly looked as if he were from a distance. He was clipping some tall wither grass that a mower was pushing down, but couldn't cut. His tool had been made from an old-fashioned bed spring support, which was shaped to the approximate loft of a 9 iron.

I was so surprised to see such a beautiful swing so many miles from a golf course that I went down for a closer look. He had a rag wrapped around the sharp edges of the grip end to protect his hands. Sometimes

102

he'd swing one-handed, and part of the time he held on with two hands. When using both hands, strange as it may seem, he used an overlapping grip, which in principle and detail was exactly what I saw Harry Vardon use when I got to England.

The grass he was clipping lay close to the ground, in about the same position as a golf ball would be placed. To get the maximum effectiveness out of each swing, he ran the bottom front edge of his implement parallel to the ground for several inches. This twelve-year-old, on a remote island in the Pacific, was using excellent golfing form, was employing the correct grip, and was also following through with *The Basic Movement*.

Choose the swing most natural for you

I have kicked myself many, many times for having lost the photographs I took of that boy, for they would have shown exactly what I mean by the naturalness of the swing. In their absence, I am including some specially marked photographs to illustrate the path of the club in proper relation to the ball and the ball's intended line of flight. Depending on your stature, you should assume one of these three positions most natural to your body:

(1) *"Upright"—the path of action for a tall person.*

(2) *"Medium"—for a person of medium build.*

(3) *"Flat"—for a person of short stature.*

You might better understand this matter of having the path of stroke in proper relation to the ball and its

How to Swing

(2) What is your swing type? Is it "upright"?

Note: *The tilt and turn of the body in this picture has been sufficient to assist in positioning the club parallel to the intended line of ball direction.*

How to Swing

(2–Cont.) *Is your swing "medium"?*

Note: *To "meet" the middle ball the body has turned more than in the preceding picture.*

How to Swing

(2–Concl.)* *Or is your swing "flat"?*

Note: *To have the plane of the swing match with the ball farthest away, the body twist is more pronounced than in the preceding picture. The progressively increased "spiraling" effect of the trousers in these three pictures tells the story more completely.*

---

* The same stance has been used in all three of these back-swing positions.

intended direction, if you were to picture what would happen if a ball were tethered in a shoulder-high position. It is easy to see how the resulting stroke would be practically horizontal. Now, if the ball were lowered to the ground, the horizontal path would become changed into more of a vertical or upright stroke. In whatever position the ball is placed from the body and feet, there automatically becomes a preferred path in which the club is best swung. Hence, each person should be typed according to the pattern of stroke considered most suitable to his individual physique.

Problem-saving pointers on your swing

Although the terminology calls for a natural swing, there are many people who, unlike some inhabitants of Pago Pago, cannot get into the proper swing naturally. The difficulty seems to lie in the downward and through parts of the swing. I have used these six pointers as my basis for solving this problem with others, and you might find it worth your while to check these through point by point.

(1) Be sure that you are well practiced in the proper lofting and dispatch of the ball— *The Basic Movement.*

I would like to go on record with the statement that many shots are spoiled by "trying to keep the head down," when the real cure for this ailment is learning how the club loft raises the ball. Putting *The Basic Movement* into practice disposes of at least 99% of the head trouble.

(2) Never practice the backswing only. Always make a completed swing.

It has been my observation that too many adults practice just the backswing, and by so doing, rarely realize the importance of exercising the muscles and joints essentially required to ease down the remaining speed of the club head after ball impact. It is as necessary to absorb the club head speed with muscular ease at the finish of the through swing as it is to generate club head speed during the downward part of the stroke previous to impact with the ball. Adults are especially referred to in the foregoing, because they, by trying to direct their learning through the mind, are apt to subordinate their imagination. Children, however, let fly with everything they have in a free play of imagination when swinging a golf club or anything else. If you stop without completing the forward movement of your swing, you are not following through in a natural movement. You are not exercising your muscles as you should, and you are not developing the proper habit pattern of swinging. Therefore, even though a pause may be required to fix your attention on finishing your swing, take it, and always deliver through to a logical completion of every full swing you make.

(3) Remember your head has to rotate with the movement of the club, rearward in the backswing, and forward with the follow-through on to the finish.

Here we have one of the most misunderstood functions of the golf swing; for it is most commonly stated in the text and teachings that the head must be kept still. If what the great champions did and are doing is to be considered correct, there could be no statement further from the truth. Head-lifting is seemingly a major problem to the rank and file of golfers. But keeping the head still or down is not the cure. The head moves during the golf swing, but it must move properly. The proper movement is rotation. I have some photographs of Sam Snead later that show how his head rotates and thereby aids free arm and figure movement.

If you wish to determine definitely how much and in what way the head of any leading player moves, do the following:

(1) Take up a position in front of the player and at right angles to the intended line of ball flight.

(2) Bring the fork between the thumb and index finger of either hand before one eye.

(3) Fold the index finger so as to make a small peep hole.

(4) Through the peep hole, focus your eye on the player's head, preferably his nose.

(5) Check the nature and amount of head movement that takes place during the ensuing stroke; and any doubt about whether his head moves will very readily be cleared up. Repeated study will show the rotating nature of the head movement.

109

**(4) Realize there must be continuity be-
tween the ball and where you intend it
to go.**

Most leading players study very carefully the target
they are aiming for. In fact, the better they play, the
more their eyes take in how the ball will best travel to
where they would have it go. In this regard, they differ
sharply from the duffer, who usually takes a hasty look
and consequently has but a vague notion of where the ball
is to go. I discussed this point with Babe Ruth, when we
were together in the gallery at the 1947 P. G. A. Championship.

"Some hit and hope," he said. "The champions hit
and know."

"Does that account for your pointing to the place
where you got that much-needed home run in the World
Series at Chicago?" I asked.

"Well, yes," he replied, "but I was lucky to get a
ball that suited the spot."

**(5) Remember that maximum club-head
speed requires a free flow and no block-
ing at impact.**

Rather than swing at the ball, try to swing through
the ball. The speed of the backswing is never so great
as in the reverse direction. This is true even though the
club head is slowed down in overcoming the inertia of the
ball by approximately forty feet per second in the follow-
through stroke of a drive of 200 yards. As noted earlier,

when Olin Dutra won the U.S.G.A. Championship at Merion in 1934, he attributed his success to a piece of advice tendered him by a former champion, Willie Mac-farlane, who, in a practice round, pointed out to Olin that he was quitting at the ball. Whether you aspire to be a professional or are merely trying to improve your game, hit through, and don't quit at the ball.

(6) Realize that the golf ball is highly resili-ent.

When a tennis ball is thrown on the floor, the under-side flattens out. Since the reaction accounts for the ball's rebound, it becomes easy to establish that the same thing occurs when the golf ball is struck by the club. This cor-responding deformation and recovery accounts for take off and flight of the golf ball. As a matter of fact, the golf ball "contracts" to a diameter of one and one-quarter inch on the face of the club in a 225-yard drive. The golf ball has a tremendous amount of stored-up energy, and it is very willing to go. It doesn't want to be shoved or pushed. So swing through it and allow the stroke to come to a natural finish without restraint of any kind.

Remember, too, that the ultimate is to have the en-tire attention trained on the ball with definite continuity as to where you want it to go. To reach this sublime state, learn well *The Basic Movement*. And learn how to grip, how to aim, and how to swing. Then, by sys-tematic practice, commit each to habit. Have each step as natural as the use of your knife, fork, and spoon. Playing golf will then be as easy and enjoyable as eating.

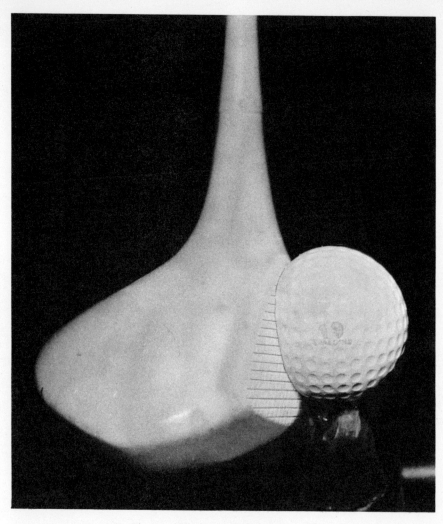

How to Swing

(3) Here is the real purpose of the golf swing. This action picture, taken by Dr. Harold E. Edgerton with his stroboscopic camera, clearly shows the contraction of the ball and the likely rapidity of its reaction. The more fully this action and reaction of the ball is understood, the better the sense of swinging the club is developed. (Dr. Edgerton is the co-author, with J. R. Killian, of Flash! Seeing the Unseen by Ultra High-Speed Photography, *2nd Ed., Charles T. Branford Co., Boston, 1954.)*

112

Points to Remember

- 1. Make the address flow from the results of the motions of taking aim.

- 2. Handle the club in the address so that it fits in with the intended swing path for the line of play.

- 3. Swing naturally once you assume the position that fits your body.

- 4. Complete every full swing. Never practice backswing only.

- 5. Swing through the ball.

- 6. Rotate your head with the movement of the club.

- 7. Commit these elements to habit so you can devote your full concentration on the ball.

- 8. Disregard any well-meant but inexpert advice.

8

From Practice to
a Round of Golf

*Y*OU now approach the danger period. You have assimilated the elementary requirements of the correct grip, the preferred way of taking aim, and the natural swing. You thoroughly understand and can properly execute *The Basic Movement*, and you muscularly know that the club face loft raises the ball. You are ready to put these essentials to practice on the golf course.

Now try your wings

It is right here where so many stumble; for up to this time the development of the fundamentals has been largely a mental one. You are now prone to divide your attention between some phase of the swing and the ball. This is a critical time. Here's why.

The only time when an individual can, with the hands, do more than one thing at the same time is when the hands are separated. Now, in making a golf stroke, the hands are united, and great care has been exercised to have them so. Therefore, as the hands become the common denominator for the entire body, which similarly has been trained to respond, every scrap of attention must be trained on the ball. You must concentrate on where it is to go and how it's going to reach the objective.

Earlier I had told how some of the great players went about taking aim, making their swing flow in a smooth, continuous sequence. They had developed their actions to a point of habit, requiring no more attention than walking, running, or any other everyday kind of thing. When at their best, they were no more aware of their swinging movement than Babe Ruth was when he made his historic World Series home run. All question or doubt on this point was conclusively resolved for me by one of the great players of today, who won an important tournament by nine strokes from a representative field with a record score. He attributed his victory to his undivided attention on the ball from the first drive to the last putt.

Stay on the ball!

What I urge you to do now is to find out how well your practice of the fundamentals is going to serve you in a practical direction. In taking a tee shot, for example, I recommend you apply yourself in the following manner:

(1) **Visualize the shot.**
(2) **Tee the ball according to the shot: down-wind—tee high, against the wind—tee low, etc.**
(3) **Take hold of the club selected for the shot.**

From here on there should be a sharp difference between the elementary practice of the past and its application. For a practical description, I would like to write out what the player is thinking to himself at this point.

"Well, here's the ball. That's where it is to go; here's testing to see if this feels right—and off she goes!"

The associated actions will, of course, be placing the club face to the ball, taking aim, the waggle or address, and then the swing. But get this—you should arrive at these things in much the same manner that you would throw a stone or ball at a target.

The point is to develop your swing into the sublimely happy state in which it responds naturally. It must, for you have to apply your entire attention to the ball and where it has to go. Remember this too—never go back into an analysis of the swing or of any other detail unless there is some repeated error. Believe it or not, no one is perfect. In fact, there never has been a championship won without some degree of imperfection in many shots made by the winner.

Any error that you could make on the golf course can be traced to a faulty execution of one of the fundamentals we have covered. But at this stage of your game, above all, avoid trying to analyze individual errors. You'd do much better to confine your attention to the ball and where it has to go. Then, only after you have made a sustained effort at carrying this out, should you go back into swing corrections. There's an old saying, "You cannot whistle and chew wheat." Applied to the golf stroke, one's undivided attention must sooner or later be trained on the ball.

Points to Remember

- 1. Practice the fundamentals of grip, aim, and swing so they become habit.

- 2. Visualize the shot.

- 3. Select the proper club.

- 4. Give your undivided attention to the ball.

- 5. Do not analyze any one phase of your stroke unless there is some repeated error.

Getting Accuracy
into Your Shots

*A*LL players strive for accuracy — not the kind erroneously thought to come from the suppression of power, but that which produces the maximum force with a minimum of effort.

Where do we get power without forsaking accuracy?

During my association with the game, it has been interesting to note how each generation of players has succeeded in applying more and still more power to the ball without any serious loss of direction or distance control. This achievement I am sure springs from their continued development of a dynamic sense of balance.

Among the leading players of today there are several fine examples of balance in action. Perhaps it could be rightly said that Sam Snead excels in this respect. To show how he operates, reference is made to four pictures taken of him. The first is the position of address, and each of the other three is at key points in his swing. The yardstick forced into the ground alongside Sam's right leg is to emphasize the following:

(1) *He does not shift his weight laterally in his backswing.*

(2) *Through balance and freedom of movement, he obtains extra power from the use of his feet and legs.*

(3) *His return of the club to the ball is bound to be more accurate, because he shows no appreciable weight shift in the backswing.*

(4) *His weight progresses toward the left side in order to suit the "flattened curve" path the club head should take immediately following impact with the ball.*

(5) *His forward movement of weight provides for the added width of the arc made by his club head in the through part of his swing, which, incidentally, is at least six inches wider than in his backswing.*

119

Photo by Alex Brenne

How Sam Snead Shoots for Accuracy

(1) Note the space between the inclined yardstick and Sam's right leg.

Photo by Alex Brenner

How Sam Snead Shoots for Accuracy

(2) The left foot action gives the impression of a weight shift; but reference to the space between the right leg and the yardstick proves otherwise. The spiral-like twisting of Sam's shirt and trousers shows the tilt and turn action since the position of address in the preceding picture.

How Sam Snead Shoots for Accuracy

*(3) This picture, taken "on the way down," shows the
forward thrusting of weight.*

How Sam Snead Shoots for Accuracy

(4) Here the weight has been transferred almost completely to the left foot. To grasp the tilt and turn of the down and through parts of Sam's swing, note the spiral effect again in his clothing.

123

*(6) He provides, with ease, for the progressive
slowing down of the spent speed of the club
head.*

Although they were not taken with a yardstick for
reference, I have a similar set of pictures of Ben Hogan.
With them, and the aid of a protractor, it is easy to prove
that Ben maintains substantially the same amount of weight
on each foot in his backswing as he does in his position of
address to the ball.

There are two schools of thought on the subject of
weight change. The old school is typified by Paul Run-
yan, who in his heyday used to make a marked transfer
of weight to the right in his backswing. The newer
school has gained in popular practice ever since the late
Abe Mitchell demonstrated how you can obtain extra
yardage from a balance of weight in the backswing and
a thrust of power of the right leg in the down and through
swing. The technique originated by Mitchell, and so well
exemplified by Snead and Hogan, has the advantages of increased distance and better control of ball direction.

The mathematical advantage of modern club design

Ben Hogan has stated that he prefers to keep the ball
in the same relative position to his left foot with all clubs
and all distances. Most other players play the ball progressively further back in going from the long to the
shorter shots. The only change Ben makes is to move

his right foot closer toward the left one as the shots get shorter. Thus, he maintains a fairly constant weight distribution in his address and backswing.

What this adds up to in Ben's case might well be called a mathematical advantage. With fourteen clubs in a set, he has but fourteen separate foot positions to take. He requires fewer moves than the player who plays the ball farther back as he progresses from long to short distance shots. This second method might conceivably amount to twenty-eight separate positions.

Modern club design simplifies the game by reducing the number of positions the player must assume in addressing the ball. I have included a series of diagrams that will show you the differences between the old- and new-style woods. Don't be frightened by the mass of statistics, for many of them remain constant. I have included them for your own information.

Let's start with the drivers. Both old- and new-method drivers are the same in all respects. You would address the ball and swing at it in the same manner with either club. The upper figure, .937″, is the distance between the center of the shaft and the ball. Note how that figure remains constant in all the new-method woods. It varies in all the old-style woods. The constancy of this figure permits the golfer to use each wood with the same stance.

The lower figure is the distance between the center of the shaft and the point of impact. This changes in all the new woods and remains constant in the old. It is here that I have accounted for the differences in club loft.

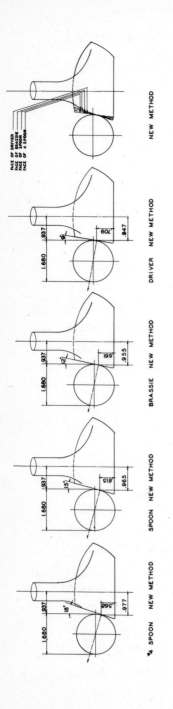

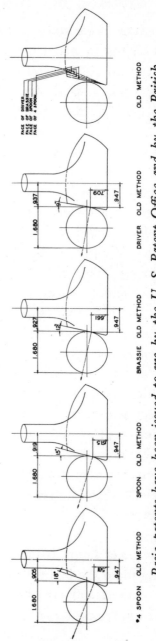

Basic patents have been issued to me by the U. S. Patent Office and by the British and Australian patent offices on the novel principle contained in my new method of club design. A comparison of their respective measurements on this page will convey the difference between the new and the old methods.

All you now have to do is hit the ball, using the same stance and the same swing for each shot. The club itself will do the rest of the work. The old method required a different position for each shot, which caused the golfer no end of trouble.

Let me remind you that your golf clubs are a set of scientific instruments, each capable of performing a certain specific job. If you can employ each club with the same *Basic Movement,* and if you will permit the loft of the club to do the work, your game cannot help but improve.

The first time the principle of advanced design, illustrated in the same drawings, was built into golf clubs was back in 1931. To me it was most gratifying that players who that year won the U.S.G.A. Open, the British Open, and the P.G.A. Championships each used clubs incorporating the newer design. This came as no surprise to me; for anything leading to standardization of stroke-making usually results in a more effective use of the muscular power of the human being. This means more distance with better accuracy.

Balance in modern club design

When the ball is struck with a club, the club head has a tendency to rotate around its center of gravity. This would cause the shaft to spin in the player's hands and throw the shot off his line of aim. Depending on where the center of gravity is located, the club's impulse to turn will be lessened or increased. A golf club, unlike a tennis racket, is not symmetrical in shape. And since it is not evenly balanced, it is best counter-balanced by localized weighting or its equivalent in shape compensation.

I have included Sketches 1 and 2 to give you some idea of the basic balance design of the conventional wood club. It has been proven by driver machine results and by player testing that the best performance with conventional type wood clubs comes from an unequal weight distribution forward and rearward of the central axis of the shaft (the center line in Sketch 1). Note that 67% to 70% of the overall weight of the rough-turned head is rearward of the center line, while 37% to 40% is forward. Likewise, tests have shown that the best distance and direction results are produced from wood clubs where the basic design disposes slightly more of the wood head weight forward, rather than rearward, of the center line of the club face (Sketch 2). Not all clubs embody such proportions. Certain models are more popular than others; and the fortunate users of clubs of sound design have the best means of developing the soundest form.

Balance your backswing

I am strongly in favor of body, leg, arm, and hand actions that do not require any weight shift in making the backswing. Here are my reasons:

(1) *The rotation of the head is continuous and in complete sympathy with the backward and forward movement of the club—no sway sideways, and practically no up-and-down movement.*

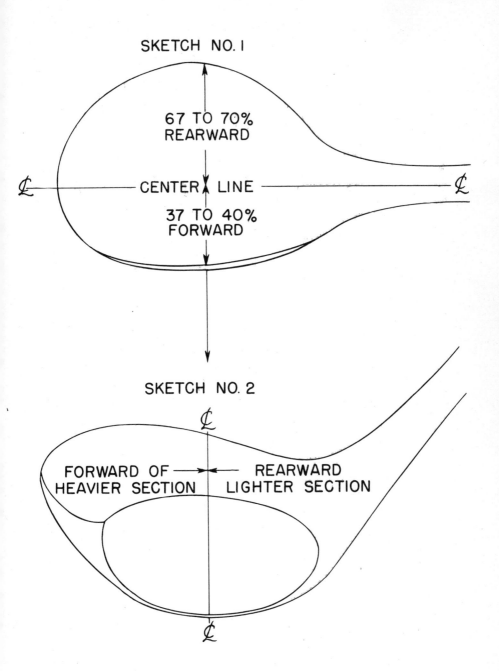

SKETCH NO. I

67 TO 70%
REARWARD

₵ ———— CENTER LINE ———— ₵

37 TO 40%
FORWARD

SKETCH NO. 2

₵

FORWARD OF →|←— REARWARD
HEAVIER SECTION   LIGHTER SECTION

₵

129

(2) *The maintenance of initial weight distribution provides for a more effective transmittal of muscle power and weight influences, thereby generating more club head speed for greater distance. At the same time, it simplifies control for better direction.*

(3) *Weight stability complements* The Basic Movement *or "flattened curve" path that the club head should travel immediately following ball contact. This insures a true backspin, without which the ball's flight becomes limited and erratic.*

This flattened curve path is another means of describing the follow-through the golfer makes after impact with the ball. When *The Basic Movement* is being properly employed, the path of the club can be likened to a curve that is flat on one end. To appreciate fully the influence of this wider action "through the ball," you have to understand that any contraction after impact is the direct result of an earlier slowing down of the club head. This error is usually traceable to faulty lofting of the ball, accompanied by an undue shifting of weight to the right side.

Points to Remember

- 1. Force need not be sacrificed for accuracy.

- 2. The fewer positions you take, the greater your chances for accuracy.

- 3. A balance of weight in the backswing aids in both power and accuracy.

- 4. Modern club design helps the golfer attain power and precision by standardizing positions and properly balancing clubs.

Perfecting Your
Hooks and Slices

A PUPIL of mine, having had a bad slice for many years, found his distance was getting shorter and shorter. He said to me, "Do you think my slice can be cured?" When I told him yes, he said, "O. K., if you can cure me of it in one week, I'll give you a hundred dollar bonus." It was a Saturday when we went to work. After completing his game the following Saturday, he came to me and said, "Victor, this hook is costing me money.   I'll pay you another hundred if you'll *guarantee* to cure it."

Let your hooks and slices work for you

Slicing and hooking problems are common.   Ben Hogan tells how close he came to an early retirement several years ago because of an uncontrollable hook.   The beginner often finds himself battling a slice.   Both of these ills are largely individual matters; and for me to analyze *all* the conceivable causes of your hooks or slices would be impossible.   I will say this: If your shots are not going straight, you are not executing some phase or phases of the fundamentals we have already covered.   I would strongly suggest a thorough review of these fundamentals with particular accent on grip and on *The Basic Movement*.   This chapter deals with understanding the factors causing a ball to hook or slice and with how you can incorporate the intentional hook or slice into your repertory of shots.

First, play it straight

The subject of this chapter brings to mind my billiard teacher, Joe Andreoli.   Besides being an expert in that field, he was a most successful trainer of athletes in many widely different sports.   Among his charges were the one-time great heavyweight champion boxer, Peter

Jackson, and George Towns, who was probably one of the greatest world champion scullers of all time.

Joe had that particular ability to get to essentials and the happy knack of imparting knowledge to others. In one of my early lessons, I learned that, of the great variety of shots there are in billiards, the hardest to perfect is the straightforward one in which the ball is struck without any semblance of sidespin. He went into considerable detail to explain how holding the cue, taking the correct stance, having a proper bridge, and cueing the ball for a true stroke all entered into the execution of this, what he considered to be, the most important shot to master. From this, all other billiard shots can easily be developed.

Before he would allow me to attempt any regular shots, I had to demonstrate my ability to hit a ball straight up the table, let the cue follow through freely, and have the ball, on its return from the end cushion, squarely contact my cue tip. As in billiards, so it is in golf. For in the latter game, playing a straight shot is most difficult of all, and is the basis for all others.

It only spins when you make it spin

Often in golf the terrain dictates that the shot should be a hook or a slice. In order to get back on the fairway, your recovery shot may best be played by slicing or hooking the ball. For those of you who have become proficient in the fundamentals, there follow the most successful methods I know for understanding, training, and developing control of intentional hooks and slices. As far as actual stroke-making is concerned, there are but two things that cause the ball to take on sidespin and force it to take a curved flight. They are: (1) the angle of the club face during contact and (2) the path and speed of the club face during contact.

To get the feel of how these two things work, take hold of a ball—on what might be called its north and south poles—with the thumb and finger of the left hand. Then, with the palm of the right hand, stroke across the back of the ball. Doing so away from you will cause the ball to take on a right-to-left rotation, and stroking toward you will cause it to turn in the opposite direction.

Having seen and felt how the ball rotates, take any club; and, holding it with the right hand down near the head, do the same thing. This very action at the moment of contact is what causes the ball to take on either a right-to-left hook spin, or a left-to-right slice spin. (The right-to-left flight was formerly called a "pulled" or "draw" shot.)

Leave the feet out of this

As you stroke the ball away from your body, your trunk probably has a tendency to turn away with the backward part of the stroke. If so, let it. If, when you extend the action, your right foot draws back, allow that too; for both are natural partners in carrying out the eventual right-to-left curved flight of the ball. Let the right foot advance as you stroke toward the body for a

HOOKS AND SLICES
(1) How to cause hook spin.

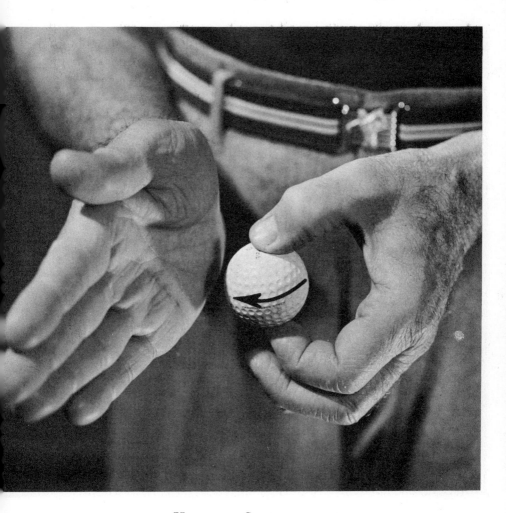

HOOKS AND SLICES
(2) How to cause slice spin.

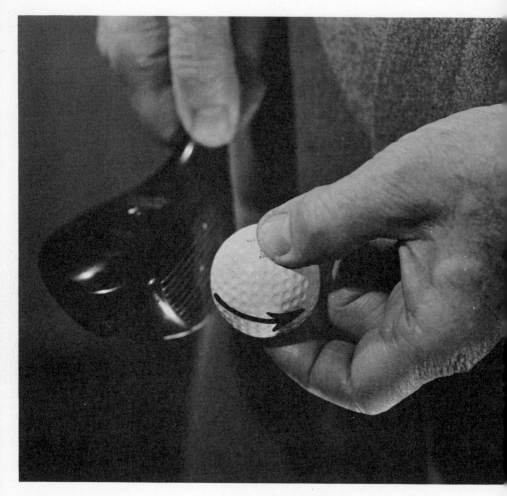

HOOKS AND SLICES

(3) For hook spin rub the ball from the toe toward the heel.

Note: *This is a good antidote to slicing.*

HOOKS AND SLICES

(4) Sliding the club face from the heel toward the toe will cause slice spin.

left-to-right rotation of the ball. Above all, do not expect to have a ball hook or slice merely because you place your feet in some pre-determined position. This foot positioning is frequently advocated in books on golf instruction. Pay little, if any, attention to where the ball should be placed in relation to the feet. Contrary to the common belief, you should put the ball forward for a hook and back for a slice. To assist you in understanding how you should position your body for each kind of shot, I refer you to the sketch on page 141.

The relationship between the ball and the left foot in both the hook and the slice pictures are substantially the same. This is as it should be, because the application of power depends primarily on having more of the body weight behind the ball. The only difference in the ball-to-left-foot line is accounted for by the fact that it is better to meet the ball a little earlier when slicing than when hooking.

The references in these sketches to the left foot, to ball positions, and to the line of take-off are not intended to promote any deliberate attention to the feet. Moreover, I want to clear up existing misunderstandings that cause improper pre-positioning of the body. This has confused many who have tried to acquire the ability to play controlled hooks and slices. As in tennis or other ball games, the feet automatically respond to the hands in whatever the latter may be undertaking. If it's a "cut" shot in tennis, the right foot, as a natural partner of the right hand, moves forward. For a "smash," the right foot moves back in direct accommodation of the hand action

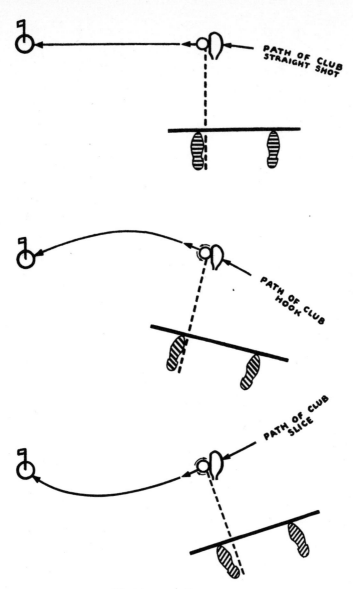

HOOKS AND SLICES

(5) Although it may look otherwise, the ball and hole-flag positions are the same in each instance. If the club face is squared to the objective, the prescribed paths for each kind of stroke will, with the corresponding foot positions, produce the indicated sliced, hooked, or straight results.

for applying the front of the racket to the top of the ball.

It is the angle of the club face and the path of its travel that causes the sidespinning of the ball. And, therefore, having visualized the nature of the intended curved flight, the player should then concentrate on taking aim and proceeding with the stroke in like sequence, as he would do in any other shot.

The left-handed player, left out so often, should consider all references to the left foot as the "front" foot.

Points to Remember

- 1. The straight shot is the hardest of all.

- 2. The angle and speed of the club face during contact causes the curved flight of the ball.

- 3. Concentrate on the face of the club, rather than your feet.

- 4. Practice for control.

11

Temperament and Touch in Putts

*T*HE putter is the golf-er's tool for accuracy within inches. Your tee shot must only be accurate within fifty yards, the average width of a fairway. Shots to the green must range within a twenty-yard width. But the putt has its accuracy requirement narrowed down to four and one-quarter inches, the width of the hole. Quite obviously, there must be a great amount of precision in the club designed for that purpose.

How to select a putter

The first thing to look for in a putter is true face alignment. If the face surface is untrue, as was the case with Bob Jones' "Calamity Jane," don't buy it. Test the putter you now own with a straight edge. If you find it is not flat from one end of the face to the other, don't use it. It will only be the source of heartache.

Look for a putter that is easy to line up; and in this regard, pay particular attention to the top line of the face. Make sure it is true and visible for its full length. It is also advisable to have all rectangular lines of its full length square to the face. You will find it much easier to square up or line up a putter that has no curved lines to deceive your eyes.

Try to choose a putter that has an even amount of material on both sides of the center line of the shaft. The resulting evenness or balance will reduce to a minimum the tendency of the putter to turn or twist at the moment of impact.

I might surprise you by mentioning that there is a third sense involved in the art of putting. You are already aware of the senses of sight and touch; but have you ever considered the importance of the sense of hearing? A friend of mine hadn't, until one day when we were playing in a rainstorm. I had loaned him my raincoat, equipped with a hood. He missed a short, exasperating putt; and he explained to me that he couldn't understand it. His putting game was way off, for no apparent reason.

144

He was finally convinced that his game was not off, but that he couldn't *hear* the shots. It ruined his accuracy.

Maybe he never really was convinced; I'm not sure. He might have been looking for an excuse. Then again, it was raining so hard he might not have wanted to continue the argument there. He was also suffering from a real spirit-dampener—he was losing money on top of it all.

Select a putter with a good "ring" or "ping" to it, and your accuracy will improve. It is significant to note that the putters which have produced the largest volume of sales during the past thirty years have been those with the higher tonal note.

Perhaps you're putting poorly

Since putting amounts to about 50% of your game, half your golfing ills can be cured by some serious study on the green. You cannot solve putting problems permanently by purchasing new putters—neither can you solve them by the "smash and replace" technique. I can't say that you will improve by emulating the style of a more fortunate duffer. Many are convinced that putting is controlled by a supernatural force, and that their success or failure is determined at birth.

Just as it is with everything else, you can improve your putting only by understanding and practicing the fundamentals. This will require a study of club design, grip, aim, and swing, as well as certain exercises.

Putters come in all sorts of different sizes, shapes, weights, and colors. They differ from other irons in their more vertical and, generally, smooth face. In selecting a putter, be sure it has a comfortable "feel." Beyond that, it becomes a matter of personal taste. Whatever type you select, be careful to position your hands so the palm sides line up parallel with the face of the putter. Do this in taking hold of the putter in preparation for the stroke. By this means, the putter face becomes a true extension of your hands, particularly the front sides of the fingers.

Your sense of aim must be keenly developed through practice; and your eyes will have to be trained to pick out minute details that will influence the distance and direction of the ball's roll to the hole. All good putters have one thing in common—their eyes are directly over the ball when they take their position for the stroke, as well as when they are making the stroke.

The stroke in putting is tempered because of the short distance involved. You are not primarily concerned with power; but you are still very definitely concerned with distance and direction. *The Basic Movement* is still employed. This shot does not involve loft. But the proper negotiation of *The Basic Movement* will insure the follow-through that so many golfers neglect while putting.

Pressure-putting with a pro

I would choose Walter Hagen as the greatest pressure-putter I have ever seen. Since his method was very sound, from the mechanical standpoint, and had all the

146

Walter Hagen, master of all he surveys.

147

elements of simplicity, I will take his procedure as an example.

As Walter came to a green—even before looking at what lay between his ball and the hole—he would take in the general contour of the green. Unlike many others, who look the line over either from the ball to the hole or vice versa, he would pick out the high point or points of the green to determine its prevailing slope. Walter would hold his putter with a reverse overlap grip (the index finger of the left hand over the little finger of the lower hand), and would take up his position over the ball. His eyes would then seek out the line for the ball to make to the hole.

In the case of a fifteen- or sixteen-foot putt, he would split up the distance into four parts and then proceed to study each section separately. By stopwatch count, he invariably spent more time on the final two sections than on the earlier ones. And since the slopes influence the ball more noticeably as its speed slows down on the way to the hole, this extra time he took on the last part of the putt was quite understandable.

By this singular method of studying his shot by sections, his sense of feel worked in marked sympathy with what his eyes picked up in the way of slopes and their influence on the ball to be played. Should the surface slope show a left-to-right ball influence, you would see his putter, which he would have held up from the green surface to roughly a horizontal position, faced accordingly to the left. Later on, should there be a reverse slope, his sense of feel would respond, and he would move the putter to match the incline.

When he was all through with his separate estimates of the several sections of the putt, he would arrive at what he felt was the correct overall angle for the ball to start on. Down would come the putter blade to the ball at this chosen angle of direction. He would then take one final look to take in the distance; and upon the return of his eyes with their best estimate, he would stroke the ball.

The records may show a lower average number of putts per round by some player other than Walter Hagen. But I don't think any champion holds the edge over Walter when it comes to holing a championship-winning putt when the chips are down. As an example of the complete composure that his method developed, I will set down what Walter told me about his winning the British Open Championship in 1924 at Hoylake.

An example of perfect composure

With a round to go, Walter was tied at 224 with Ernest Whitcombe, an early starter. Shortly after Walter started the last eighteen holes, word reached him that Whitcombe had taken a dismal 43 strokes for the first nine. This caused Walter to let up a little, and he had three sixes in his score at the turn. Three holes later, information came to him that Ernest had staged a great recovery on the back nine and had finished with a grand total of 302 strokes. This jolted Walter into a realization that he would have to beat par for the remaining seven holes.   This was a tough assignment under fair conditions, and it was made even more difficult by the high winds on that eventful afternoon.

Here is Walter's description to me at the Biltmore Hotel on the night of his return from England:

I wasn't proud of my second shot to the twelfth green; but I holed a sloping twenty-five footer for a birdie and was still in business.

The wind whipping in off the Mersey fooled me; and I was trapped with my tee shot on the short thirteenth.   I nipped the ball out of the sand and up into the green, got down in one putt for a par, and was safely through a tough one.

The fourteenth is a par 5.   To reach it in 2 I could either try for the green over the whins and rushes or play safe.   I went for the green and made it for another birdie.

Number fifteen was critical.   It was a tough par 4, with a gale blowing right into my face.   My drive was O.K.; but the ball was lying close.   The caddie offered me a spoon. Brother, if you turn down a British caddie's selection of a club, you'd better be perfect with the one of your own choice.   To myself I reasoned, "If I'm going to win, a driver it's got to be!" I got off a fine shot and rubbed it out by three-putting.

Well, I'll skip the sixteenth and seventeenth and bring you along to the eighteenth, where the hole from tee to green was framed by the crowd. I really cut one loose from the tee. The newspapers called it the longest drive of the tournament. I couldn't say about that, but I knew it was my best of the four rounds.

On coming up to the ball, I debated with myself whether to "cut the legs" out from under it and spin it to a quick stop or just to toss one up and let it die out naturally. I looked around at all those people and said to myself, "They've got to have the shot played sometime." So I drifted one up and it stopped rolling two feet past the green on a sparsely grassed spot that was sort of soft.

When I got up to the ball, I looked it over and decided I definitely wouldn't chip to the right side of the cup, because the green sloped in a tricky way and was extra keen from that side. So, where do you suppose I stuck it? Exactly! To the right of the hole. The papers said it was anything up to twenty feet. Actually, it was about six!

I looked it over carefully and it seemed I had about one chance in five of making it drop.

Then, as I stood there sizing it up, the thought hit me: "Gee! I can beat this guy in a playoff tomorrow anyhow." I touched her just right and the ball snuggled right down into that hole.

Principles of precision putting

As already intimated, Walter Hagen's methods contained the essentials, as well as the elements, of simplicity for good putting. Let's review his technique step-by-step. I will follow these with other supplementary ideas of proven use and influence. Remember, it takes less time to do all these things than it does to write about them.

> *(1) When taking hold of the putter, be sure to have the palm side of each hand lined up parallel to the face of the putter.*
> *(2) Cultivate a stroke that accurately returns the putter face to the same angle at which it was placed when you originally addressed the ball. (I refer you to the illustrations which show you how to cultivate a true putting stroke by using a yardstick to practice at home. Be sure to have your eyes directly over the ball position.)*
> *(3) As you approach the green to be putted on, take in the high and low points. By so doing, you will learn the general contour.*
> *(4) Look for the actual line of travel your ball will best take to make the hole. In so do-*

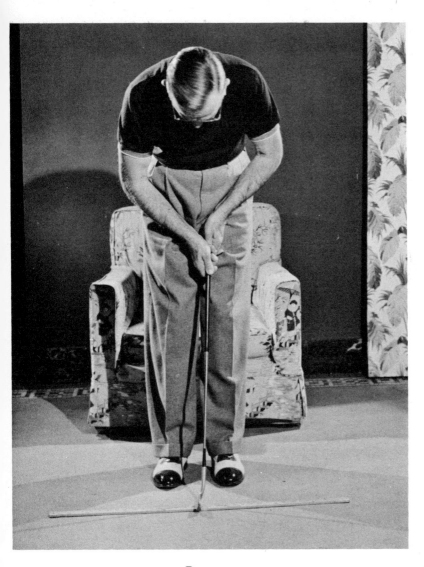

PUTTING

(1) Address. Regardless of whether the feet are apart or together as shown, it is of vital importance to square the putter face to the immediate line along which the ball is to roll. Training and testing over a yardstick will be useful.

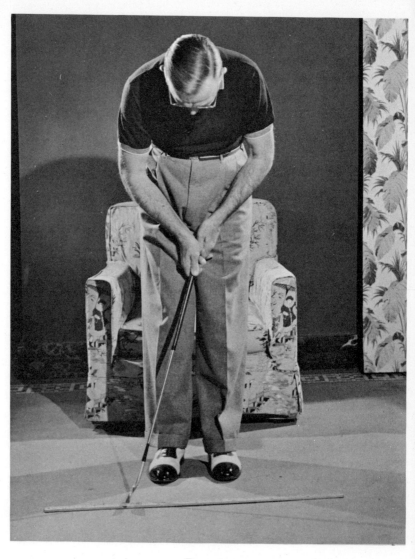

PUTTING

*(2) Back stroke.   To move the putter back and forth
to the ball position is principally a combined wrist action.   Continue checking the putter face for square-
ness over the yardstick.*

154

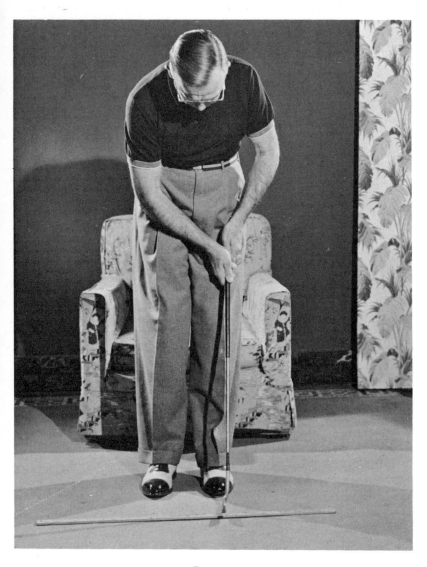

PUTTING

(3) Through stroke. To insure that the ball will roll true, it is advisable to have the putter "follow on" squarely. Because the shaft angle is inclined away from the vertical, this is best accomplished by having the hands and arms travel forward with the putter head as shown. What happens immediately afterwards is a matter of individual choice.

ing, you will observe whether the "line" conforms to the general contour or is influenced by any local condition. If you can picture the way water would flow over the surface, you will know which way the ball will roll.

(5) Be sure to place the putter face square to the line selected for the ball's immediate take-off.

(6) Having established the direction by placing the putter, take a look from ball to hole to pick up the distance. Then, when your eyes have returned to the ball, with the sense of required force, stroke the ball on its way.

Except to state that Walter Hagen looked over the line from the ball to the hole in several separate parts, the foregoing contains the methods he so successfully employed in putting.

There are, of course, many other contributing factors that will help you improve your putting. For the most part, they come from keen observation of the influencing elements. For instance, if you're on a seaside links or a course that is exposed to the more rigorous weather, observe whether the trees or plants have been forced to lean in one direction by the wind. From this you will know that the grain of the grass on the putting greens will more than likely follow the same general direction.

This matter of grain is a very important consideration for successful putting. Become ready to sense its presence. Observe whether or not the surface looks shiny. Usually, when there is a pronounced grain, the mowing has the effect of clipping off the leaves of the grass, which exposes the fibrous runners. This causes the shiny appearance. The surface will be fast in the direction of the shine and slower from the other side.

You should be able to tell whether the putting surface is hard or soft by your first few steps on the green. The harder the green, the faster the ball will travel. You can also recognize the speed of the green by color. If, for instance, there is poor drainage, the blades of grass will appear yellow. This putting surface would be faster than the one of a healthy, green color, because the weak grass does not offer so much resistance to the ball.

The reference to the healthiness of the grass reminds me of another item that you should be keen to observe: the slope or relative flatness of the putting surface. Grass grows best where there is both surface and subdrainage. The golf course architect usually sees to it that the sites chosen for putting greens already have, or can be easily adapted for, suitable drainage contouring, and still fit in with the natural surroundings. Such being the case, a flat surface for a putting green is a rarity, and is only possible where the soil is of a light, friable nature, to allow the easy passage and absorption of moisture.

Therefore, you will hardly ever find a perfectly straight putt—unless, of course, there is one up or down a direct incline toward the hole. Since a straight putt is such a rarity, how can you best tell the degree of slope in order to allow for the proper amount of "borrow" and speed? In addition to the conventional methods of determining the slope, you should look carefully at the way the metal cup has been set in the green. It is the greenkeeper's intention to have the flag stick as perfectly upright as possible. When the hole is cut, there will be an obvious difference in the amount of soil showing between the top edge of the cup and the grass surface of the green. Observing the thick and thin layer of soil above the metal cup will help you in arriving at the eventual line and speed requirements of the ball's course into the hole.

Aside from the essentials for developing a sound putting stroke and using the powers of observation to sharpen your feel or putting touch, there is an additional item that has proven of considerable value. To highlight this, I will recount a talk I once had with the late Ted Ray, who won the U.S.G.A. Open Championship at Inverness in 1920.

When in Scotland in 1921, I asked Ted how it was he had become such a fine putter. He told me he had been very much impressed by a statement made to him that a big man—he was well over two hundred pounds—usually was clumsy on the greens and rarely became a good putter. He said he took the comment quite seriously and decided he would prove the idea wrong. Realizing that billiards and golf were not so dissimilar, since in both games the player has to deal with a stationary ball, he decided to take up billiards as one step in the direction of improving his putting. He said, "You know, as my billiards improved, so did my putting. But the thing I believe helped

158

me most was the trick I developed of bouncing and balancing a golf ball on the face of my putter."

He would drop the ball on the face of the putter and hit it up again and again to different heights. Then he would change his pace; and each succeeding hit would be lighter and lighter, until finally he would have the ball come to rest on the face of the putter. We subsequently had a round together on the King's Course at Gleneagles; and Ted, as we walked along from the green to the next tee, demonstrated how he used to keep his putting touch in shape.

It was his opinion that his putting touch became as sensitive as if he were practicing music with a violin. He went on to say, "There are several things involved in getting a good touch. But I'm sure one of the most important is to feel the weight of the ball and to know how it reacts to the weight and force with which the putter strikes it. That is why I decided on bouncing it up and down as much as possible." I could mention many, who, by doing as Ray did, have improved their results in putting.

The mental attitude toward putting is something hard to come by with most golfers. With a chosen few, this is the phase of putting that is inborn; most of us never develop it. But when you miss the short one, or when you strike the twenty-five footer just right and she rims the cup and dribbles off to one side—and you still have the courage to smile—either you a master of the mental attitude of putting or you're playing the wrong game.

159

Points to Remember

- 1. Have your eyes directly over the ball while taking position and during the actual stroke.

- 2. Line up the palm sides of your hands parallel to the face of the putter.

- 3. Observe all the elements that will influence the roll of your ball.

- 4. Practice the Ted Ray method of getting the feel of the ball.

12

How to Keep Track
of Your Game

*M*Y family was about to
move near the Pacific
Ocean. Several weeks before the big move, my father
called my older brother Ernest and me together. "Now
when you get out to the shore, you boys will have to know
how to swim. So, if you will put some cushions on the
floor and lie on them on your stomachs, I'll show you
what to do when you get in the water. As you go to push
off,"—and showing us at the same time, he proceeded—
"put your hands with the palms together out in front of
you. Then, as you glide forward, turn your palms outward and try to push the water backwards with a sweeping

movement of your arms. Also, try to push the water backwards with the soles of your feet."

He had us practice the hand, arm, and leg movements quite frequently, and I well remember his saying, "Now you won't have any trouble with your swimming." He was right. When I went into the water for the first time, I had no trouble reaching the opposite side of the pool.

This was a most valuable lesson in my learning how to teach golf. It taught me that learning something that involves a new muscular action requires a preliminary understanding of the purpose of those movements. This must be followed by adequate practice in order to develop the movements to the point of involuntary reaction or habit.

Learning how to teach

As far as I can remember, the first time I used *The Basic Movement* in teaching was on the old Royal Sydney Golf Club course. Lord Hampden, Governor of New South Wales, had failed dismally one day in getting his ball to clear a pond on the way to the fifth hole. Disturbed by this and other similar experiences, he came to the club the following day with the avowed intention of conquering what he said was just a complex. He bought a box of new balls, and with me in tow, carrying his bag of clubs, went straight to the pond. As I took each new ball from its paper wrapping and put it down, he promptly knocked it into the water. His supply ran out after a dozen.

Kids are apt to recognize tense situations, and in this one it occurred to me to say, if he did not mind, that I thought I could help him. On receiving his permission to do so, I took two balls of my own from my pocket, and putting one opposite the other so as to have one serve as a marker, said, "Now, if I play this as I think I will, you will be able to tell that *the club sole grazes the turf after meeting the ball. But when you try, your club, by not following the slope of the ground, hits the turf before the ball.*

Fortunately, I got the stroke properly and the ball cleared the pond. Furthermore, from the ball placed opposite, he was able to see the club sole had taken the turf after meeting the ball. Flushed with this success, I then told His Lordship we boys had practiced so much we could sort of hop-skip-and-jump the ball across the water. Luckily enough, the ricochet shot worked too. Whereupon he asked if I would mind getting the balls I had played so he could use them to try again. After I retrieved the balls, he put both across successfully. We were both happy, especially myself, since he paid me more than double the amount I had expected.

These two experiences have had a profound effect on my teaching the game. As you review the previous text, you will recognize my entire philosophy on teaching golf as an expansion of these two principles. Understand the principles by which the club projects the ball, and practice this *Basic Movement* until your actions become habit.

This is something you can learn on your own, and I can guarantee that your score will improve and you will get more fun out of the game.

To see ourselves as others see us

> O wad some Pow'r the giftie gie us
> To see oursels as others see us!

When he wrote these penetrating words, the great Bobby Burns, himself a keen player, surely must have had golfers in mind; for that is one of the most important things to every devotee of the game.

Most people who see the game played can tell good form from bad. Beyond this, it is not difficult for each one to select a successful pattern to achieve. But many golfers' inability to see themselves as others see them is where their practicing tends to "gang aft agley."

The professional's ability to mimic the pupil's actions in attempting to pick up the correct stroking becomes an invaluable aid in teaching. People cannot help but learn by seeing how they look. Boxers carefully study the films of their previous fights. Football teams go over their movies time and again. When you can see for yourself what you're doing wrong, rather than just being told, you will understand and improve much more rapidly.

Another way to see yourself as others see you is to practice before a mirror. This I would strongly advocate. Like any form of practice, it should be directed by a professional so the exercise will fit in with a definite swing pattern. The body action of a tall person requires more tilt in the turning movement of the back and through parts of the swing than the body action of a short person requires. Hence, each individual should be shown the exact nature of the body twist and related hand positions he should strive for when practicing before a mirror.

Regardless of stature, each person can, to his great advantage, see that his head rotates without undue sidewise or up-and-down motion. Accomplishment of this important factor can be greatly aided by having a strip of adhesive tape put on the mirror in an up-and-down position to check whether the head rotation is carried out without any swaying movement.

It would be opportune to set down the conclusions arrived at, after many years of study, on the influences of head movement in the golf swing.

First, the head must move. There's no such thing as "keeping the head still," as so many golf books advocate.

Next, the head action, in the backswing as well as for most of the through swing, is a rotation, rather than a side-to-side movement. There have been a few exceptions; but my records compiled over many, many years prove convincingly that the most successful players are those whose head rotation up to contact with the ball operates pretty much within the scope of the original position taken at the time of address to the ball.

In addition to practice before a mirror, a very simple way to check whether or not the body and head movements are performed properly is to use one's shadow. All that is necessary is to throw a ball down to serve as a marker.   Then place yourself so that your head shadow covers the ball.   Make the backswing and see if the shadow has shifted.   If it does show movement to the right or left side, practice to get its rotation centered over the ball. This shadowgraph can be a most informative and helpful procedure that will help promote and produce the much desired dynamic sense of balance.

How to keep in good golfing trim

Since there are so many muscular movements to be unified in the makeup of the golf swing, and because the everyday way of life—except in rare instances—does not bring the exact combination into use at the same time, the human figure is apt to lose some of its desired flexibility. To offset this condition, and at the same time keep the golfing muscles in tone, several simple exercises are recommended for home practice.

If, during the practice of these exercises, one has in mind that they are intended to be a part of a working whole, much more good will develop than would otherwise be the case.   In this regard, it is advisable to picture the purpose of each exercise and to know how it will contribute to the whole swing.   In each case, refer to the explanatory photographs.

EXERCISE 1   *Hands, Wrists, Forearms*

These will encourage the right placement for gripping the clubs.   Additional strength will develop for power and control of the club when swinging.

EXERCISE 2   *Hands, Arms, Body*

Recommended for development of the desired body action during the swing. Particularly recommended for women. Next to learning how to loft the ball, this is the biggest single difficulty adults have in learning golf.

EXERCISE 3   *Punching*

Same as above. Recommended for men.

EXERCISE 4   *Body, Arms, Legs*

Advocated by Sam Snead for limbering up, for getting the swing underway, and for development of the dynamic sense of balance. The fact that his feet are close together automatically discourages any undue tendency to sway in the backswing.

EXERCISE 5   *Balance in Motion*

Development of the tilting and turning movements of the body. A club could serve just as well as the yardstick in these pictures. The most important thing in doing this exercise is to be sure the ends point downward to where a ball would normally be teed up or played from. This applies in both the back and forward action.

167

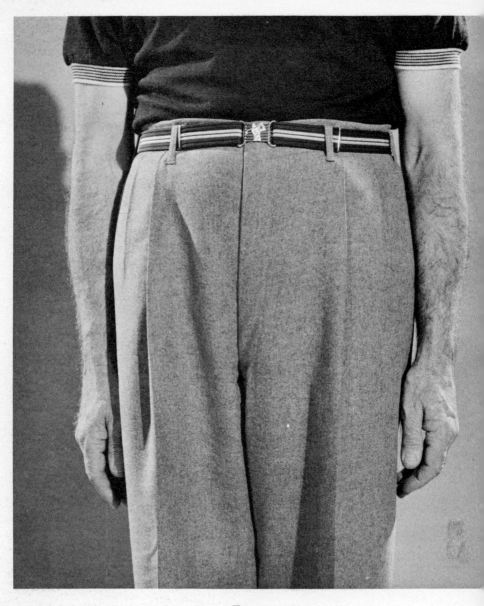

EXERCISE 1

(1) Hands open.

168

EXERCISE 1

(2) Hands closed. The inward curving toward the wrists is important to form the channel for the club to fit into. The closing and opening exercise will strengthen the fingers and forearms.

169

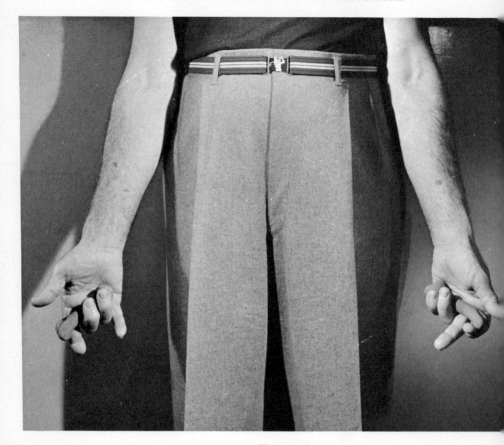

EXERCISE 1

(3) Rubber dog bones. Notice where the thumbs and grooves are placed for gripping.

Note: *Strength can be gained by squeezing tennis balls; but they hinder, rather than help, the important shaping of the hands.*

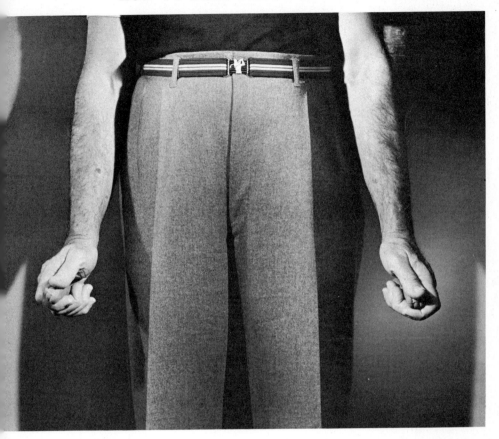

EXERCISE 1

(4) Rubber dog bones with the hands closed. Notice how the wrists are cocked. Doing this while gripping promotes freedom of movement.

EXERCISE 2

This triple exposure illustrates the back-and-forth hand-slapping exercise for the development of body action and head rotation.

EXERCISE 3

*This punching exercise develops the coordinated move-
ment so vital to making the whole swing.*

Photo by Alex Brenner

EXERCISE 4

(1) Sam Snead practicing with his feet together and his club held at arm's length.

Note: *The white stripe on Sam's hat shows the companion head movement.*

174

EXERCISE 4

(2) Swinging the club back without the hand-wrist action.

175

EXERCISE 4

(3) Swinging club down and forward without the hand-wrist action.

176

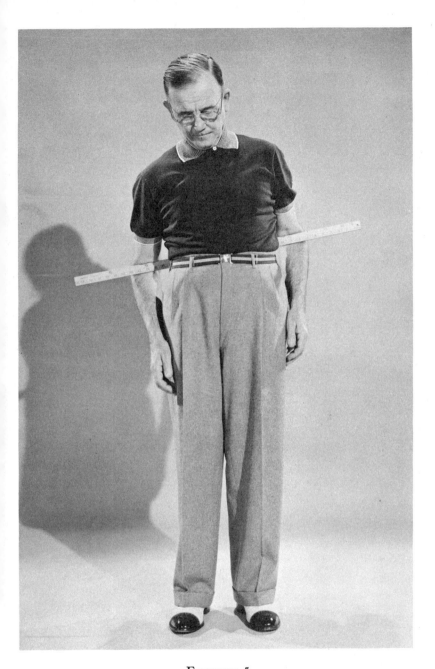

EXERCISE 5

(1) Tilting, with a yardstick behind the back and in front of the arms.

177

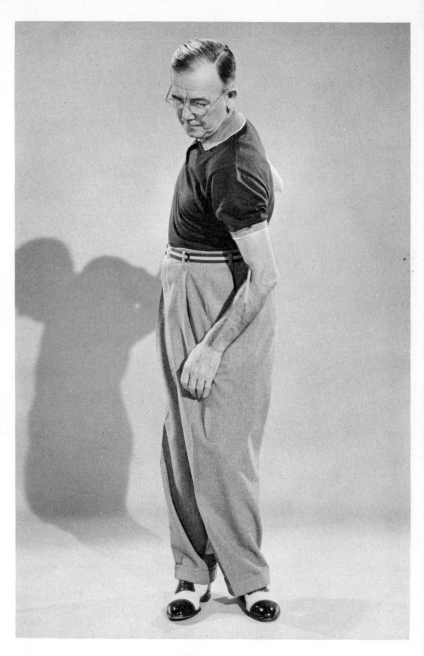

EXERCISE 5

(2) Tilting and turning right.

EXERCISE 5

(3) Tilting and turning left.

179

The off-season would be the best time to practice these exercises. It is then when the muscles are prone to lose their tone and the figure gets stiffened up. The exercises, of course, can be carried out systematically during the playing season. And, by keeping the muscular responses alert, much conscious or deliberate attention to detail is thus avoided. If by practice the correct impulses become habit, you do not have to worry about anything but the ball and where—from shot to shot—you would have it go.

Confusion in terminology

Since one of the primary purposes of this book is to communicate such knowledge as has come my way during more than a half-century, I feel it will be of interest to devote some attention to certain supposedly key words that have become used almost universally in teaching the game. I am firmly convinced these words have not achieved their intended purpose.

I will select just two examples: "pivot" and "relax." Per the medium of Webster, we are taught that the word "pivot" has to do with a revolving movement around a fixed center, such as might be carried out in drawing a circle with a compass. As it is common knowledge that the shape of a golf stroke is not circular, by elementary geometry we know there cannot be a fixed center for its execution—and hence no "pivot."

In the teaching of golf, the word "pivot" is more accurately used when describing the movement of the *body* in making a swing. Based on results from its use with individual pupils and in group instruction, I would state quite definitely the results have been most disappointing. What generally happens when a student is directed to pivot is that he will start turning his figure away from the ball in a shoulder-level or somewhat horizontal plane. Because this movement does not produce the proper upward path for the club, the hands quite instinctively become separately engaged. So, instead of there being a cooperative effort of all the working parts, a conflict of purpose develops and the stroke as a whole becomes distorted.

With the foregoing in mind, it would be my suggestion that, when individuals are confronted with the word "pivot," they substitute the idea that the figure should *tilt and turn* in making its getaway from the ball. Of course, there should be a reverse tilting and turning of the body in the downward and through parts of the swing.

If you will think back to the chapter on aiming, you will recall a specific reference made to the preferred sequence for getting the swing underway. In this connection, I would emphasize that, if the eyes have become trained to travel from the ball along the line of intended direction and likewise back to the ball, this training will automatically promote the correct tilting and turning of the body. Thus, it can develop the united action of all working parts in the whole swing. So, it is my recommendation that *tilt and turn* take the place of "pivot."

I firmly believe that there is misuse of the word "relax," in connection with making a golf stroke. One

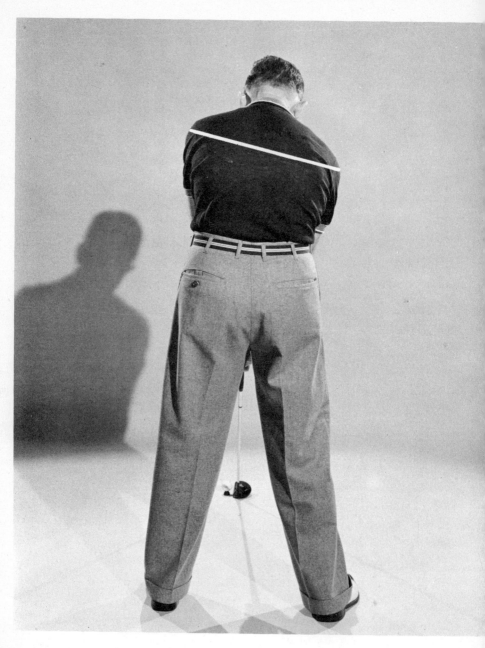

GOLF TERMS AND THEIR PURPOSE
(1) Tilted shoulder position at address.

182

GOLF TERMS AND THEIR PURPOSE

(2) Tilted and turned shoulders in the backswing.

GOLF TERMS AND THEIR PURPOSE

(3) The reverse tilted and turned position at the finish.

has only to note the tense expression on any good golfer's features when a full-sized drive is being made to know the speed—which, for a carry of 225 yards, approximates 140 miles per hour—does not come from a state of relaxation. For sure, there is a marked difference in the free movements of the working parts of the good players, as against the stilted-to-stiff actions of the rank and file who do not play the game so well. However, the difference is not one between being relaxed and tense. There's more to it than that.

As a main source of power, the good golfer makes the best possible use of his larger body muscles. He also draws on the muscles of his legs, arms, feet, and hands as auxiliaries—the latter being used more particularly as a supplementary means of accelerating the speed of the club head. With the good golfer, the spontaneous use of the combined muscular forces becomes translated into motion. This motion—plus the weight of the body and of all the moving parts—is transmitted to the club, and in turn to the ball, per the medium of the hands, whose responsibility it is to control the club for a square impact of the club face with the ball.

In sharp contrast, the duffer is prone to have disconnected muscular movements—sometimes a series of them—that rarely become blended into a united effort. To superimpose on such people the idea that they should be "relaxed" does not meet the situation. What has helped in the majority of cases of this sort is the recognition of the fact that there is a vast difference between the construction and the application of the golf swing, interwoven with which is freedom of movement.

I am fully aware that anxiety promotes mental tension. But to relax this tension it is necessary that its cause be determined. I do want to state that it is my firm conviction that the use of the word "relax," in connection with making a golf swing, should more generally be replaced with *freedom of movement.* Be calm, be mobile, would be my advice; but *don't try to be "relaxed."*

There are other words found in fairly common use in the teaching of the golf swing that do not achieve the desired purpose. As indicated earlier, I will not take up any further discussion along these lines and will conclude this chapter with the suggestion that the teaching section of the Professional Golfers' Association might well go further with the work they have in hand of simplifying and standardizing the terminology of the game.

Points to Remember

- 1. Understand the necessary muscular action.

- 2. Practice necessary muscular actions so they become part of a working whole.

- 3. Practice before a mirror.

- 4. Check your head movements by observing your shadow.

- 5. Exercise during off-season.

- 6. Substitute *tilt and turn* for "pivot."

- 7. "Relaxed" is a condition of the mind, not the body.

13

Totaling Up the Score

*W*HEN I was a mere boy, I had a temporary position at the Australian Golf Club, which afforded me my first opportunity to give lessons. It was not until a new, man-sized job at the Royal Sydney Golf Club was thrust on my youthful shoulders that I became fully aware of the responsibilities that went with the club professional position.

I remember quite easily how my mind shaped up on this subject of teaching. First, to be a good example to others, it was important to have a sound golf stroke. Secondly, it seemed I should be able to play well enough

to beat the best player in the club. Thirdly, it was necessary to be able to detect the errors of individuals and communicate the knowledge of their corrections.

By diligent practice, I acquired what I believed to be
a sound swing. In any case, it was good enough that by
my fifteenth birthday I was able to concede a handicap
to the best player in the club.

Back near the turn of the century, literature on golf
was quite limited; but I read it all, and some of it many
times. However, then, as now, much of the information
was of conflicting nature, and, for the most part, dealt
with effects rather than causes. Since there was no clear-
cut pattern on methods of instruction, I decided on a plan
of keeping progress records for each person to whom I
gave lessons. This became an indexed card file. Among
other things, such as age, handicap, and suitability of equipment used, these cards had provision for noting the faults
of each pupil. There was classification of the more or less
common golfing errors, including topping, slicing, hooking, smothering, and shanking. Opposite each item, space
was provided for noting the cause of the trouble, the correction, and the pupil's progress.

By studying these records, I was led into conducting
a research program. As a part of this research program,
many methods of instruction were set up and careful
studies were made of the results. The opportunity of
testing certain theories and of obtaining comparative results was fortunately provided by my having two college
groups to teach. One group was made up of girls and
the other of boys. Each group belonged to a different

school and was in a different location. I decided to divide each group into two separate squads, with each squad made up so the ages would be comparable.

For the purpose of the test, my plan was to teach one squad of girls and one squad of boys by "eye"—the process of demonstration for imitation—and to direct the effort of the other two squads through the "mind." In other words, the first group was shown *how* and the second group was shown *how* and told *why*. The second group made by far the better progress.

My next step was to find out why the first group did not perform or score so well as the second. To learn this I took up positions at separate points on the golf courses where the respective groups played. It did not take long to realize that the form or style of the individuals in what I will call "Group How" was not sustained so well as that of "Group Why." It had done as well on the practice fields, but not so well on the golf course. The comparative failure in the stroke-making was particularly noticeable when the girls had a water hazard to play over and the boys a tall hedge to negotiate.

What particularly went wrong with "Group How" was that, with hardly any exceptions, each individual gave way to the primitive impulse of trying to help the club get the ball from the ground. In the terminology of the game, they "scooped at" instead of "following through" to allow the loft of the club to get the ball into the air.

Not long after this experience with these young people, I repeated the same kind of experiment with an adult group at an officers' military camp, with substantially the same result. This proof of learning by mental direction, rather than by imitation, was very convincing to me back in those early years of the present century—so much so that subsequently I made it a point, when describing *what* had to be done, always to explain *why* it was necessary. Youngsters require less detail than oldsters. But, as with all things motivated by the mind, there never can be too much knowledge. This is particularly true when physical effort is called for—more especially in tournament or championship play.

This book would take far too long to write and would become too tediously voluminous if I were to set down in detail the nature and results of all the tests made in my search for the best method of helping others develop good golf form. Therefore, I will only summarize the conclusions arrived at from my research program and correlate the results obtained from tabulations of the indexed records kept of individual pupils.

The one thing that became crystal clear from research and record-keeping was that fully 90% of the errors of both omission and commission were traceable to total or partial failure muscularly to comprehend *The Basic Movement*. It was only when the fact that the club face would take care of getting the ball off the ground had been put into practice that the player-to-be could properly apply the necessary attention to controlling the *direction* and the *distance* the ball was to travel.

Even with those who sliced—and of the middle- to long-handicap group, slicers predominated—it was found their side glancing of the ball off line and consequent loss of distance came mostly from this same basic mistake of trying to help raise the ball.

Even recent checking has confirmed this fact that 90% of all golfing ills are attributable to faulty lofting of the ball. So there will follow a word picture and illustration of the simple mechanics of the correct method, the understanding and performance of which will simplify the acquisition of an effective golf swing.

Since every golf club is made with sufficient face loft to contact below the equator of the ball, and also having in mind that the golf ball is highly resilient and therefore very responsive, it is elementary that, if the club face strikes the ball below center, the ball will develop backspin and thereby take off from the ground.

Now, study the illustration that shows a 5 iron loft. Note the distance below the equator it would contact the ball. Especially take in the arrows indicating backspin and the resulting angle of ball take-off. *More particularly, be impressed with the path the club should travel immediately following the impact with the ball.*

Because the mechanics of lofting the ball are simple and are so readily understandable, it is likely that many readers will feel they have little doubt about their proficiency in carrying them out. However, *since it is a matter of record that no more than 10% of the golfers have committed the mechanics to muscular habit*, I am going to refer you back to the simple test in Chapter 2 by which it is possible for you to prove whether or not you have acquired the knack of properly lofting the ball.

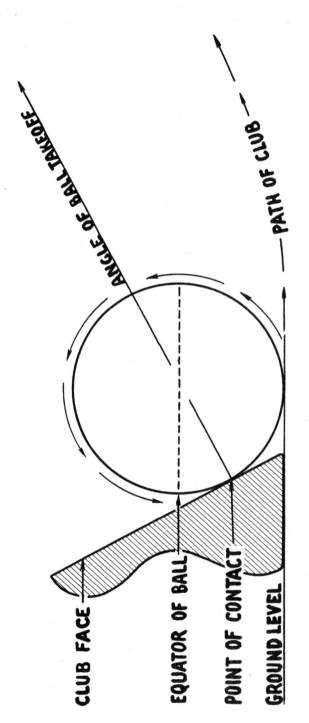

ANGLE OF BALL TAKEOFF

PATH OF CLUB

CLUB FACE

EQUATOR OF BALL

POINT OF CONTACT

GROUND LEVEL

193

If you fail, here are the things to check on:

Be sure, when placing the club to the ball, that its sole is level with the surface.

Be sure, when making the stroke, that the club sole slides forward along the surface, at and immediately after contact with the ball.

The realization that the loft of the club face raises the ball will soon come to you. Acquire the habit of this small-scale exercise by repeated practice. It will go a long way toward your putting the principle into effective use in actual play, and it will solve many of the faults in your stroke-making which have as their origin the primitive impulse of trying to help the club raise the ball. Remember always, the player's responsibility is to control the direction and distance of the ball, and that the desired elevation of the ball is built into the respective clubs of his set.

Index

197

INDEX